TO

Steven

from

D1461848

BEST.
GAGS.
EVER!

Published by Prion
An imprint of The Carlton Publishing Group
20 Mortimer Street
London W1T 3JW

Content previously published as *Laugh? I Nearly Shat!* in 2007

ISBN: 978-1-85375-919-2

10 9 8 7 6 5 4 3 2

Typeset by E-Type

Printed and bound by CPI Group (UK) Ltd, Croydon, CR0 4YY

BEST.
GAGS.
EVER!

Compiled by
Alan Buxton

PRION

INTRODUCTION

There seem to be very few things in life that are both good for us and which we enjoy doing.

Laughter however may be one of those things. Not only is it good for the soul, it can relax you and reduce stress, it boosts your immune system, it can relieve pain, reduce aggression and even improve your blood pressure.

Laughter is indeed the best medicine, although you probably shouldn't rely on it if your doctor has prescribed antibiotics.

Also if you have a condition that causes you to keep guffawing without a break 24 hours a day, 365 days a year, it may not be quite so good for you.

But generally speaking most of us could probably do worse than to laugh a little more often than we currently do.

On the other hand the business of actually making people chortle is not always that easy. It is surprisingly difficult to get up in front of an assembled audience and get a few chuckles out of them as almost anyone who has ever tried doing it will surely confirm.

We should therefore salute anyone who possesses this amazing talent. And this little volume is a celebration of some of the greatest comedy performers, writers and other joke-smiths of the past 100 years. It is a collection of some of their greatest moments and most memorable one liners. Either it will remind you of some extraordinary comedy performances or it will introduce you to some of the most incredible talents in the history of entertainment. It is quite literally the Best. Gags. Ever!

Obviously, that is a slightly subjective judgement. Nevertheless, if you agree that the likes of Groucho Marx, Spike Milligan, Tony Hancock, Morecambe and Wise, Tommy Cooper, the Two

Ronnies, Victoria Wood, Les Dawson, Billy Connolly, Peter Cook and Dudley Moore, Monty Python, Bob Hope, Jack Benny, George Burns, Gracie Allen, Rita Rudner, Alan Partridge, Bill Hicks, Joan Rivers, Woody Allen, Steve Martin, Frank Carson, Linda Smith, Jeremy Hardy, Jerry Seinfeld, Larry David, Richard Pryor, Zach Galifianakis, Jimmy Carr, Frankie Boyle, Sarah Millican, David Mitchell and Harry Hill knew (and/or continue to know) a thing or two about crafting a decent joke, you could indeed currently be holding the Best. Gags. Ever! in your hands!

Yes, some of these people are so good at being funny they are still making people laugh even though they are no longer around. Groucho Marx was born in 1890 and died in 1977. And yet, despite the apparent handicap of having been dead for nearly 40 years, he is still instantly recognisable and remains capable of making audiences around the world laugh their socks off.

That is the magic of a brilliant performer with fantastic material. And this book is packed with the very best gags ever from the world's very best comedy stars ever.

So read it, enjoy it, share it with your friends and – whatever you do – don't forget to have a good laugh!

Hello.
I can always tell straightaway if an audience is going to be good
or bad... So, goodnight!

Tommy Cooper

IN THE BEGINNING...

In the beginning, the universe was created. This has made a lot of people very angry, and is generally considered to have been a bad move.

The Hitchhiker's Guide To the Galaxy

Ali G: But what has God ever done?
The Bishop of Corsham: He made the world.
Ali G: What? He made the world?
Bishop: Yes.
Ali G: Did he?
Bishop: I can only tell you what I believe.
Ali G: So you saying God made the world? And since then he's just chilled?

Ali G

And God said, "Let there be light". And there was light, but the Electricity Board said He would have to wait until Thursday to be connected. And God saw the light and it was good. He saw the quarterly bill and that was not good.

Spike Milligan

ABDUCTION

My mother used to say to me when I was younger, "If a strange man comes up to you, and offers you candy, and wants you to get into the back of his car with him... GO!"

Woody Allen

ABUSE

Child sex abuse seems to have happened to so many people, but after I was born, my parents were hardly interested in having sex with each other, let alone me.

Garry Shandling

ACCIDENTS

If you fall out of that window and break both your legs, don't come running to me.

Groucho Marx

Dr Kilmore: Just as I thought. You fell on your coccyx.
Francis Bigger: I did not! I fell on my back.

Carry On Doctor

Inspector Dreyfus (having just accidentally shot his nose off): Don't just stand there, idiot; call a doctor! And then help me find my nose…

Return of the Pink Panther

Fielding (finding himself injured): Blood! That should be on the inside!

Bananas

Reports are coming in that an elephant has done the ton on the M1. Motorists are advised to use great caution and treat it as a roundabout.

The Two Ronnies

A man falls down a flight of stairs and somebody rushes over to him and asks, "Did you miss a step?" "No," he answers, "I hit every one of them!"

Milton Berle

Another motoring flash: on the A30 this afternoon a tanker-load of bleach on its way to the West Country overturned on a notorious accident blackspot, turning it immediately into a notorious accident whitespot.

The Two Ronnies

As soon as I went into the skid I tried to remember the safe driving manual, which says, "If you go into a skid, turn in the direction of the skid." Which is like saying if a guy throws a left hook at you, you lean into it.

Bill Cosby

ACCOUNTANTS

Max Bialystock: You're an accountant! You're in a noble profession! The word 'count' is part of your title!

The Producers

The company accountant is shy and retiring. He's shy a quarter of a million dollars. That's why he's retiring.

Milton Berle

ADULTERY

Last night my wife met me at the front door. She was wearing a sexy negligée. The only trouble was, she was coming home.

Rodney Dangerfield

Eighty percent of married men cheat in America. The rest cheat in Europe.

Jackie Mason

I think my husband is having an affair with his secretary, because I would find lipstick on his shirt, covered with white-out.

Wendy Liebman

Men would like monogamy better if it sounded less like monotony.

Rita Rudner

Never tell. Not if you love your wife... In fact, if your old lady walks in on you, deny it. Yeah. Just flat out, and she'll believe it: "I'm tellin' ya. This chick came downstairs with a sign around her neck: "Lay On Top of Me Or I'll Die." I didn't know what I was gonna do...."

Lenny Bruce

Chandler: My dad slept with Mr. Gribaldi.
Monica: Who's Mr. Gribaldi?
Chandler: DOES IT MATTER?

Friends

ADVERTISING

I'll tell you the commercial they'd like to do, if they could, and I guarantee you, if they could, they'd do this, right here. Here's the woman's face: beautiful. Camera pulls back: naked breast. Camera pulls back: she's totally naked. Legs apart. Two fingers, right here, and it just says, "Drink Coke." Now, I don't know the connection here, but goddamn if Coke isn't on my shopping list that week.

Bill Hicks

ADVICE

My mum told me the best time to ask my dad for anything was during sex. Not the best advice I'd ever been given. I burst in through the bedroom door saying "Can I have a new bike?" He was very upset. His secretary was surprisingly nice about it. I got the bike.

Jimmy Carr

A word to the wise ain't necessary. It's the stupid ones that need the advice.

Bill Cosby

Chandler: I'm not so good with the advice... can I interest you in a sarcastic comment?

Friends

AFFECTION

My girlfriend told me I should be more affectionate. So I got two girlfriends.

Rodney Dangerfield

AFRICA

The only thing I know about Africa is that it's far, far away; about a 35 hour flight. The boat ride's so long, there are still slaves on their way here.

Chris Rock

AGE

Nice to be here? At my age it's nice to be anywhere.

George Burns

Dorothy: Age is just a state of mind.
Blanche: Tell that to my thighs.

The Golden Girls

A sexagenarian? At his age? That's disgusting.

Gracie Allen

I don't need you to remind me of my age. I have a bladder to do that for me.

Stephen Fry

I'm looking forward to being properly old: really old, so that I can lean over in a restaurant and say to my son, "You know what I just did? I just pissed myself.... You deal with it!"

Dylan Moran

I said to my wife, "If I ever get like that – y'know, mumbling to myself and shitting my pants – shoot me!" She said, "Better start running, monkey boy!"

Lee Evans

In my lifetime I saw the Berlin Wall come and I saw it go. George Burns can say the same thing about the Ice Age.

Bob Hope

When I was a boy the Dead Sea was only sick.

George Burns

It feels great to be nearly 100: I mean, for those parts of me that still have feeling.

Bob Hope

He's so old that when he orders a three-minute egg, they ask for the money up front.

Milton Berle

I'm so old they've cancelled my blood type.

Bob Hope

I'd rather have two girls at 21 each than one girl at 42.

W C Fields

Everything that goes up must come down, but there comes a time when not everything that's down can come up.

George Burns

It is said that at the age of 55 each man becomes what he most despised at the age of 25. I live in constant fear lest I become a badly organised trip to Bournemouth.

Simon Munnery

Talk about getting old, I was getting dressed and a peeping tom looked in the window, took a look and pulled down the shade.

Joan Rivers

She said she was approaching 40; I couldn't help wondering from what direction.

Bob Hope

If a woman tells you she's 20 and looks 16, she's twelve. If she tells you she's 26 and looks 26, she's damn near 40.

Chris Rock

Saffy: Mountaineers have died falling into shallower ravines than your wrinkles!

Absolutely Fabulous

I think women spend far too much money going into Boots and buying all this anti-wrinkle cream to slap on their faces to make them look younger, and it doesn't work. You might just as well slap a bit of fruit cake mix on your face, go out in the sun for two hours, then at least you've got a cake to show for it.

Jo Brand

It's a frightening feeling to wake up one morning and discover that while you were asleep, you went out of style.

Erma Bombeck

Middle age is when your age starts to show around your middle.

Bob Hope

Sophia: I'm settling my estate.
Dorothy: What estate? Your bus pass and loofah sponge?

The Golden Girls

My grandfather will be there tonight. A marvellous old chap; you'd never think he was 104 – he looks older.

Ronnie Corbett

I've got to watch myself these days. It's too exciting watching anyone else.

Bob Hope

My grandmother is over 80 and still doesn't need glasses. Drinks right out of the bottle.

Henny Youngman

You know you're getting old when the candles cost more than the cake.

Bob Hope

AGE DIFFERENCE

My girlfriend is 14 years younger than me. Cashback!

I'm Alan Partridge

I don't have a serious girlfriend and my friends give me a lot of pressure to settle down, but I'm not worried about settling down. Why should I be? I'm 29, I'm in showbusiness and, if things go well, my wife hasn't been born yet.

Arj Barker

The older he gets, the younger his girlfriends get. Soon, he'll be dating sperm.

Billy Crystal

No woman in the history of the world ever admitted she married a man for his money. How come I never saw a 17-year-old girl with a 60-year-old man who drives a truck?

Jackie Mason

AGORAPHOBIA

Ted: Maybe he's agoraphobic.
Dougal: Jack? Scared of fighting? I don't think so, Ted!

Father Ted

ALABAMA

I was born in Alabama, but I only lived there for a month before I'd done everything there was to do.

Paula Poundstone

ALCOHOL

Mrs Merton (to George Best): If you hadn't run around so much, maybe you wouldn't have been so thirsty.

Mrs Merton

American beer is a lot like making love in a canoe; it's fucking close to water.

Eric Idle

It only takes one drink to get me loaded. Trouble is, I can't remember if it's the 13th or 14th.

George Burns

I was tired one night and I went to the bar to have a few drinks. The bartender asked me, "What'll you have?" I said, "Surprise me." He showed me a naked picture of my wife.

Rodney Dangerfield

Back in my rummy days, I would tremble and shake for hours upon arising. It was the only exercise I got.

W C Fields

Charlton Heston admitted he had a drinking problem, and I said to myself: "Thank God this guy doesn't own any guns!"

David Letterman

Do not allow children to mix drinks. It is unseemly and they use too much vermouth.

Steve Allen

French wine-growers fear that this year's vintage may be entirely spoiled due to the grape-treaders' sit-in.

The Two Ronnies

Have you ever been so drunk you wet the bed? Not laying in it: just standing up and pissing on it?

Zach Galifianakis

Here's to alcohol: the cause of, and solution to, all of life's problems.

Homer Simpson

I always keep a supply of stimulant handy in case I see a snake, which I also keep handy.

W C Fields

I got my dog three years ago because I was drunk in a pet store. We had nine cats at the time. The cats started hiding the alcohol after that.

Paula Poundstone

I had to stop drinkin', 'cause I got tired of waking in my car driving 90.   .

Richard Pryor

I know what you're thinking: "You've been drinking again, Paul." No, well, yes, but I know when to stop. I know if I'm lying on my back, choking on my own vomit, I know I should only have one, maybe two, more drinks and after that I better stick to shorts.

Paul Calf (Steve Coogan)

I never drink water, the reason being, fish make love in it.

W C Fields

I once drank 17 pints of Guinness followed by a vindaloo curry. The next morning, I had the most amazing out-of-body experience.

John Dowie

I remember the difficulty in Glasgow of my father being a teetotaller – and the shame, on Saturday nights, of him being constantly thrown into pubs.

Arnold Brown

I was court-ordered to Alcoholics Anonymous on television. Pretty much blows the hell out of the second A, wouldn't you say?

Paula Poundstone

I went out with a guy who once told me I didn't need to drink to make myself more fun to be around. I told him: "I'm drinking so that you're more fun to be around."

Chelsea Handler

I'm in no condition to drive… Wait! I shouldn't listen to myself; I'm drunk!

Homer Simpson

My dad was the town drunk. Most of the time that's not so bad, but New York City?

Henny Youngman

My favorite alcohol is tequila, 'cos my brain cells sing the Mexican National Anthem as they die.

Basil White

Not one man in a beer commercial has a beer belly.

Rita Rudner

Now, don't say you can't swear off drinking. It's easy. I've done it a thousand times.

W C Fields

The main purpose of alcohol is to make English your second language.

Robin Williams

The problem with the designated driver program: it's not a desirable job. But if you ever get sucked into doing it, have fun with it. At the end of the night, drop them off at the wrong house.

Jeff Foxworthy

'Twas a woman who drove me to drink. I never had the courtesy to thank her.

W C Fields

When I was at college I was a very big drinker and I'd get nights when I'd get so pissed I couldn't remember what I'd done the night before and I'd wake up on the bus the next morning with one shoe on, no knickers and carpet burns all over my chin – where the bloke had tried to drag me out of his flat, obviously.

Jo Brand

Why is American beer served cold? So you can tell it from urine.

David Moulton

Woody: Pour you a beer, Mr. Peterson?
Norm: All right, but stop me at one. Make that one-thirty.

Cheers

You know you have a drinking problem when the bartender knows your name, and you've never been to that bar before.

Zach Galifianakis

ALLERGIES

I have a nut allergy. When I was at school the other children used to make me play Russian Roulette by force-feeding me a packet of Revels.

Milton Jones

Peanuts! What happened to peanuts? Now every bugger's allergic to peanuts! It's true; you open a packet of peanuts now and a bunch of five-year-olds in a five-mile radius slam to the floor, jabbing themselves with adrenalin!

Lee Evans

ALTERNATIVE MEDICINE

Alternative medicine: I can't see it becoming an emergency procedure. I think it's a long time before you're at the scene of a car crash and someone'll come through the crowd saying, "I'm a herbalist; what this poor man needs is marjoram." Look in the front bit of their diary. Does it say, "In the event of emergency, pick me some parsley"?

Jack Dee

AMBITION

All my life I've had one dream: to achieve my many goals.

Homer Simpson

Alex: I'm not really a cab driver. I'm just waiting for something better to come along. You know, like death.

Taxi

I always wanted to be somebody, but I should have been more specific.

Lily Tomlin

AMERICA

Give Us A Clue was made all the better by its resident expert Lionel Blair, who was particularly good at the films of Richard Gere. Who can forget the gleam of satisfaction in his eye when he was given Yanks by Michael Aspel for two minutes?

I'm Sorry I Haven't A Clue

I have just returned from Boston. It is the only thing to do if you find yourself there.

Fred Allen

Americans stick their nose where it doesn't belong more than Cyrano de Bergerac giving head.

Dennis Miller

America's one of the finest countries anyone ever stole.

Bobcat Goldthwait

I come from a small town: Incline, Nevada. It's as American as British foreign policy.

Kit Hollerbach

ANAL RETENTION

Patsy: She was so anally retentive she couldn't sit down for fear of sucking up the furniture!

Absolutely Fabulous

ANATOMY

Alice: I'm all ears. Well, not all ears. I'm face and tummy and legs and lots of other bits, including some rather private bits I only let a doctor see… except he wasn't a doctor, and later he got arrested.

The Vicar of Dibley

> If something about the human body disgusts you, complain to the manufacturer.
>
> *Lenny Bruce*

ANCESTRY

A new study has found that three million Irish men can trace their ancestry back to just one man. In his defence, the man said that he'd been drinking.

Conan O'Brien

Ah, you've got nothing to worry about there. It's the blood you're thinking about, isn't it? British: undiluted for 12 generations. No, anybody who gets any of this will have nothing to complain about. There's aristocracy in there, you know. You want to watch who you're giving it to. It's like motor oil; it doesn't mix, if you get my meaning.

Tony Hancock (The Blood Donor)

ANCIENT ROME

For ten years Caesar ruled with an iron hand; then with a wooden foot, and finally with a piece of string.

The Goon Show

Reg: All right: but apart from the sanitation, medicine, education, wine, public order, irrigation, roads, the fresh water system and public health, what have the Romans ever done for us?
Attendee: Brought peace?
Reg: Oh, peace! Shut up!

Monty Python's Life of Brian

ANNIVERSARIES

I asked my wife, "Where do you want to go for our anniversary?" She said, "Somewhere I've never been!" I told her, "How about the kitchen?"

Henny Youngman

ANTARCTICA

Bloodnok: I claim the South Pole in the name of Gladys Ploog of 13, Sebastapol
    Villas, Sutton.
Seagoon: Who is she, sir?
Bloodnok: I don't know, but obviously we're doing her a big favour.

The Goon Show

ANTI-MATERIALISM

"Imagine no possessions," sang John Lennon, who owned a luxury apartment in
New York solely to house his clothes.

Arthur Smith

ANTIQUES

It's my antique pocket watch, and it makes me look British, and I need that for
my analysis. It's a gorgeous gold pocket watch, however, and I'm proud of it.
My grandfather, on his deathbed, sold me this watch.

Woody Allen

APATHY

Some mornings, it's just not worth chewing through the leather straps.

Emo Philips

APPEAL

Ladies and gentlemen, I appeal to you – well, perhaps not all of you…

Frankie Howerd

APPEARANCE

I do apologise for looking a bit shit tonight, but I've had flu and I forgot to wash
my T-shirt… and my parents weren't very attractive.

Jo Brand

She got a mudpack and looked great for two days. Then the mud fell off.

Henny Youngman

You want to feel really handsome? Go shopping at Asda.

Brendon Burns

You look like a normal person – if you can find a normal person who wants to look like that.

Milton Berle

I don't worry about losing my looks. It's finding them on someone else that worries me.

Simon Munnery

Is it fat, bald and Scouse in here, or is it just me?

Alexei Sayle

APPLAUSE

I finally heard some applause from a bald man and said, "Thank you for clapping me," and he said, "I'm not clapping; I'm slapping my head to keep awake."

Les Dawson

APPOINTMENTS

George: I don't think I've ever been to an appointment in my life where I wanted the other guy to show up.

Seinfeld

ARGUMENT

Man: Look, this isn't an argument.
Mr Vibrating: Yes, it is.
Man: No it isn't, it's just contradiction.
Mr Vibrating: No, it isn't.

Monty Python's Flying Circus

I argue very well. Ask any of my remaining friends. I can win an argument on any topic, against any opponent. People know this, and steer clear of me at parties. Often, as a sign of their great respect, they don't even invite me.

Dave Barry

ART

Ernie: My auntie's got a Whistler.
Eric: Now there's a novelty.

Morecambe and Wise

One time I went to an art gallery where all the work had been done by children. They had all the paintings up on refrigerators.

Steven Wright

Franz Liebkind: Hitler. There was a painter! He could paint an entire apartment in one afternoon! Two coats!

The Producers

In my house, on the ceilings I have paintings of the rooms above, so I never have to go upstairs.

Steven Wright

ASHES

In the Czech Republic, some drunken friends accidentally drank their grandfather's ashes mistaking them for instant coffee. They realised their mistake when they noticed that the coffee tasted of Werther's Originals.

Have I Got News for You

ASK A STUPID QUESTION

Rose: Can I ask a dumb question?
Dorothy: Better than anyone I know.

The Golden Girls

Sybil: Are you still here, Basil?
Basil: No; I went a few minutes ago, dear, but I expect I'll be back shortly.

Fawlty Towers

Frazer: I keep a philatelist's shop.
Captain Mainwaring: How do you spell that?
Frazer: S – H – O – P.

Dad's Army

(Bill is flying a kite)
Passerby: Y'all flyin' a kite?
Bill Engvall: Nope. Fishin' for birds!

Bill Engvall

I was on the subway, sitting on a newspaper, and a guy comes over and asks, "Are you reading that?" I didn't know what to say, so I said, "Yes". I stood up, turned the page and sat down again.

David Brenner

ASTHMA

Asthma doesn't seem to bother me any more unless I'm around cigars or dogs. The thing that would bother me most would be a dog smoking a cigar.

Steve Allen

ATHEISM

I'm not an atheist. How can you not believe in something that doesn't exist? That's way too convoluted for me.

A Whitney Brown

ATOMS

Scientists have estimated that every person on earth has some atoms in their body from every other person who ever existed. Yikes. This means I have atoms in my body from Buddha, Jesus, Lincoln, Geronimo, Hitler, Attila the Hun, Lassie and Marilyn Monroe. At least now I understand my mood swings.

Tim Allen

ATTENTION

Seagoon: To try to draw her attention, I set fire to myself. It moved her. She fried an egg on me.

The Goon Show

ATTRACTION

Mrs Merton (to Debbie McGee): But what first, Debbie, attracted you to the millionaire Paul Daniels?

Mrs Merton

Mrs Fassbender: Is she prettier than me?
Dr Fassbender: Is she prettier than you? I'M prettier than YOU!

What's New, Pussycat?

Cat: I'm so gorgeous, there's a six-month waiting list for birds to suddenly appear every time I am near!

Red Dwarf

Helen (to Sam): You're almost as good-looking as Diane says you think you are.

Cheers

She has everything a real he-man would want: big muscles and a beard.

Morecambe and Wise

Things you'll never hear a woman say: "My, what an attractive scrotum!"

Jeff Green

Wouldn't it be great if we lived in a world where insecurity and desperation made us more attractive?

Albert Brooks

ATTRIBUTES

I have the heart of a lion, the eye of a eagle and the cock of a rhinoceros. Now all we need is some glue.

Simon Munnery

AUDIENCES

The audience were with me all the way, but I managed to shake them off at the station.

Harry Secombe

Y'know, you can't please all the people all the time; and last night, all those people were at my show.

Mitch Hedberg

AUSTRALIA

Interviewer: Why are Australians so good at sport?
Dame Edna: Good food and diet, open-air life, juicy steaks, sunshine – and the total absence of any kind of intellectual distraction.

Dame Edna Everage

AWARDS

Alvy Singer: What's with all these awards? They're always giving out awards.
Best Fascist Dictator: Adolf Hitler.

Annie Hall

David Mitchell (asked to come up with an unlikely Oscar acceptance speech): I'd like to thank the person who cast me as a blind, autistic, Parkinson's disease-ridden mute, for making this award almost inevitable.

Mock the Week

BAD BREATH

Do you suffer from bad breath? Well, now your problem days are over with new Quillies lozenges. If you feel down in the mouth, suck Quillies and see how it changes your life!

Radio Active

BALDNESS

I knew I was going bald when it was taking longer and longer to wash my face.

Harry Hill

I was going to buy a book on hair loss, but the pages kept falling out.

Jay London

I'm not actually bald. It's just that I'm taller than my hair.

Clive Anderson

BALHAM

From Colgate's Folly, Balham's famous beauty spot, which stands nearly two feet above sea level, the town is spread below us in a fairyland of glittering lights, changing all the time: green, amber, red, red and amber, and back to green.

Peter Sellers (Balham: Gateway to the South)

BALL BEARINGS

Ronnie B: And now a sketch about two workers in a ball bearing factory, in which I play a man who loses his bearings.
Ronnie C: And I play a man who loses his temper.

The Two Ronnies

BARGAINS

George: I'll sniff out a deal. I have a sixth sense.
Jerry: Cheapness is not a sense.

Seinfeld

BATTERIES

I bought some batteries, but they weren't included, so I had to buy them again.

Steven Wright

BATTLE OF HASTINGS

It was to one of my ancestors that King Harold, at the Battle of Hastings, spoke his very last words. He said, "Watch where you're pointing that bow and arrow; you'll have somebody's eye out in a minute."

Ronnie Corbett

BEARDS

Manny: You think I should wash my beard?
Bernard: Yes, I think you should wash it. Then you should shave it off, nail it to a
    Frisbee and fling it over a rainbow.

Black Books

BEAUTY

Beauty is in the eye of the beholder; get it out with Optrex.

Spike Milligan

BED

When you say to a child, "Bedtime; it's bedtime now", that's not what the child
hears. What the child hears is, "Go and lie down in the dark… for hours… and
don't move. I'm locking the door now."

Dylan Moran

Fielding: I was a nervous child; I was a bed-wetter. When I was younger, I used
to sleep with an electric blanket and I was constantly electrocuting myself.

Bananas

BEGGING

My dad was too proud to beg on the streets – so he used to beg indoors.

Ronnie Corbett

BEING FOLLOWED

Bush said today he is being stalked. He said wherever he goes, people are
following him. Finally, someone told him: "Psst, that's the Secret Service."

Jay Leno

BEING STOOD UP

Larry David (waiting for a call from Ted Danson and Mary Steenburgen): They
could at least lie to us. You know, call us and lie? We don't want to sit here like

schmucks. A lie is a gesture; it's a courtesy; it's a little respect. This is very disrespectful.

Curb Your Enthusiasm

BELIEF

A man's got to believe in something. I believe I'll have another drink.

W C Fields

BENDING OVER

Doctor: Can you touch your toes?
Patient: No, sir.
Doctor: Then how do you wash them, you dirty little man?

I'm Sorry, I'll Read That Again

BINGO

Then they have a bit of alternative bingo. You don't shout "House!", you shout, "Squat!"

Alexei Sayle

BIRMINGHAM

Birmingham is often described as "the Venice of the North". History relates that when Canaletto was first commissioned to paint the Renaissance splendour of the Grand Canal, Venice, he crossed the Piazza San Marco, climbed the Rialto Bridge and, gazing towards the Doge's Palace, remarked: "Bloody hell, it looks just like Birmingham."

I'm Sorry I Haven't A Clue

BIRTHDAYS

I noticed your first couple of birthdays in life and your last couple of birthdays in life are very similar. In both cases, you don't really even know it's your birthday. People have to say: "These are your friends. They've come to help you celebrate your birthday." And you need a little help with the cake blow, in both cases.

Jerry Seinfeld

BISEXUAL

I used to tell people that I was bisexual just so they'd think I'd had sex twice.

James O'Loghlin

I'm glad I'm not bisexual. I couldn't stand being rejected by men as well as women.

Bernard Manning

BLACK BEAUTY

Black Beauty; he's a dark horse.

Tim Vine

BLACK OUTS

Population researchers say there's no proof that people have more sex when the power goes out. I know I didn't have any sex during the blackout. How could I? MY COMPUTER WASN'T WORKING!

Lewis Black

BLACKPOOL

May I say what a thrill it is to be here in Blackpool again, which, as you all know, is Morecambe with O-levels.

Les Dawson

BLAME

Basil: Oh, it's my fault, is it? I thought it was your fault for falling asleep or Manuel's fault for not waking you, and all the while it was my fault. Oh, it's so obvious now I've seen the light! Well, I must be punished then, mustn't I? (Spanking himself) You naughty boy!

Fawlty Towers

Vyvyan: Vyvyan, Vyvyan, Vyvyan! Honestly! Whenever anything explodes in this house, it's always, "Blame Vyvyan!"

The Young Ones

BLIND DATE

I am a big Blind Date fan, but the contestants are a bit weird, aren't they? I wonder if they speak like that all the time? If you walk up to them on the street and asked them a question like, "Excuse me, do you know where I could buy some coal?" (Starts rotating his hips) "Well, if it's a fire you want to start, I'll light one in your chimney that's never going to go out, 'cos I'm hot..."

Sean Lock

BLINDNESS

A woman was taking a shower. There's a knock on the door. "Who is it?" "Blind man!" The woman opens the door. "Where do you want these blinds, lady?"

Henny Youngman

On my income tax 1040 it says: "Check this box if you are blind." I wanted to put a check mark about three inches away.

Tom Lehrer

BLOWING YOUR NOSE

What always staggers me is that when people blow their noses, they always look into their hankies to see what came out. What do they expect to find? A silver sixpence?

Billy Connolly

BOOKS

Little is known about Shakespeare except that he named one of his plays after a brand of cigar: the classic love story of the young blade and his frail girlfriend, Romeo and Slim Panatella.

I'm Sorry I Haven't A Clue

Ralph: Do you...er...do you like Kipling, Ted?
Ted: I quite like the fruit slice, sir.

The Fast Show

31

I've tried to inject a little intellectual substance to the conversation down the mine. I said to a fellow-miner the other day, I said, "Have you heard of Marcel Proust?" He said, "No. He must work down another mine."

Peter Cook

Eric: You could be another Brontë sister.
Ernie: But I can't sing.

Morecambe and Wise

George Bush says, "Gore's book needs a lot of explaining." Of course, Bush says that about every book.

Bill Maher

I gave my young nephew a book for Christmas. He's spent six months looking for where to put the batteries.

Milton Berle

BOSTON

I have just returned from Boston. It is the only sane thing to do if you find yourself up there.

Fred Allen

BOTTLED WATER

I feel kind of silly buying the bottled water. Maybe I'm just too Midwestern. Every time I go into a store, I'm always like, "Hey, how you doin'? Yeah, I know you can get water free from any faucet but... uh... I want to pay for it. I'm just curious, do you have any air back there? Can I buy your garbage?"

Jim Gaffigan

BOTTOMS

Sally: Having a bottom is living with the enemy. Not only do they spend their lives slowly inflating; they flirt with men while we're looking the other way.

Coupling

My God, if her bum was a bungalow, she'd never get a mortgage on it.

Victoria Wood: As Seen On TV

BRAINS

Groucho: You know, you've got the brain of a four-year-old child, and I bet he was glad to get rid of it.

The Marx Brothers (Horse Feathers)

I used to think that the brain was the greatest organ in the human body. Then I realised: "Hey! Look what's telling me that!"

Emo Philips

I've had this brain for 30 years. It hasn't done me any good!

Abbott and Costello

Miles: My brain! It's my second favourite organ!

Sleeper

See, the problem is that God gives men a brain and a penis, and only enough blood to run one at a time.

Robin Williams

BRAS

In the last couple of weeks I've seen the ads for the Wonder Bra. Is that really a problem in this country: men not paying enough attention to women's breasts?

Jay Leno

BRAVERY

Vicar: Well, I must say, you're a braver man than I am.
Verger: Well, there's all sorts of courage, Vicar. I mean, I don't know how you have the nerve to stand up and give those sermons every Sunday!

Dad's Army

I'm a hero with coward's legs.

Spike Milligan

BREAKFAST

I always take my wife morning tea in my pyjamas. But is she grateful? No, she says she'd rather have it in a cup.

Morecambe and Wise

Jen: OK, Moss, what did you have for breakfast this morning?
Moss: Smartie cereal.
Jen: Oh, my God, I didn't even know Smarties made a cereal.
Moss: They don't. It's just Smarties in a bowl with milk.

The IT Crowd

BREAKING UP

Rebecca: What do you say when you break up with a woman?
Sam: I usually say, "I'll call you tomorrow."

Cheers

There is one thing I would break up over and that is if she caught me with another woman. I wouldn't stand for that.

Steve Martin

Mary (in desperation): Oh, John, John, talk to me. Say something to me. Say you hate me. Say I'm ugly.
John: Which?

I'm Sorry, I'll Read That Again

Tony: Alex, did you ever have to break up with a woman? What am I saying? You was married! Do you remember what you said to your wife to break up with her?
Alex: Yes, I remember what I said. I said, "Why is that man wearing my pyjamas?"

Taxi

When it's over, it's over, and I should know. I'd get into bed and she would mentally dress me.

Richard Lewis

BREASTS

I hate to see women breastfeeding in public. The baby's head obscures your view.

Sean Meo

Are you kiddin'? I know I'm ugly. My mother breast-fed me through a straw.

Rodney Dangerfield

I was such an ugly baby. My mother never breast-fed me. She told me she only liked me as a friend.

Rodney Dangerfield

If God had meant them to be lifted and separated, He would have put one on each shoulder.

Victoria Wood

Jerry: Looking at cleavage is like looking at the sun. You don't stare at it, it's too risky. You get a sense of it and then you look away.

Seinfeld

Steve: You see women as a transport for breasts!

Coupling

Who ever thought up the word 'mammogram'? Every time I hear it, I think I'm supposed to put my breast in an envelope and send it to someone.

Jan King

Y'know, God experimented with the other animals before he got around to us. You ladies oughtta thank him for creating the cow, and getting that udder idea out of his head!

Gallagher

BRITAIN

Tom Baker: Britain, Britain, Britain! Here are some facts about Britain that you might not know. Number One: Britain is a country. Number Two: Britain is called Britain. Number Five: Britain!

Little Britain

A lot of my countrymen say rude things about you, and I don't think that's fair, because I know that England will rise again. It will! It will, say, to the level of Sicily or Ethiopia.

Edna Everage

England is the only country in the world where the food is more dangerous than the sex.

Jackie Mason

If an Englishman gets run down by a truck, he apologises to the truck.

Jackie Mason

I'm English, and as such I crave disappointment. That's why I buy Kinder Surprise.

Bill Bailey

It was a typically British birth. I was three at the time. They had a strike in the maternity ward. I came out in sympathy.

Bob Hope

Jesus Christ: we know he wasn't English because he wore sandals, but never with socks.

Linda Smith

Last time I went Intercity there were a couple across the aisle having sex. Of course, this being a British train, nobody said anything. Then they finished, they both lit up a cigarette and this woman stood up and said, "Excuse me, I think you'll find this is a non-smoking compartment."

Victoria Wood

Moriarty: I see that ten years in Britain have not changed your Imperial Roman outlook, Caesar.
Caesar: True, Moriartus, always a Roman .
Moriarty: Will you take wine?
Caesar: No, thanks. I think I'll have a half of mild and a packet of crisps.

The Goon Show

My folks were English. They were too poor to be British. I still have a bit of British in me. In fact, my blood type is solid marmalade.

Bob Hope

BUILDERS

In 1926 the Queen Mother laid the first block of stone in our tenement. After a month or so the council realised she was going to take for ever, so they had to let her go and get the builders in.

Sean Lock

Hugh Dennis (asked to come up with 'bad things to say at the opening of the new Wembley Stadium'): Is it just me, or does it all feel a bit wobbly?

Mock the Week

So I rang up a local building firm. I said, "I want a skip outside my house." He said, "I'm not stopping you."

Tim Vine

I went for a job on a building site. The foreman said to me, "Can you make a cup of tea." I said, "Yes." He said, "Can you drive a fork lift truck?" I thought, how big's the kettle?

Ronnie Corbett

BULLYING

I was bullied at school – called all kinds of different names – but one day I turned to my bullies and said: "Sticks and stones may break my bones but names will never hurt me." And it worked! From there on, it was sticks and stones all the way.

Harry Hill

BUNGEE-JUMPING

I like to think of bungee-jumping as suicide for indecisive people. It's like a tester, isn't it?

Jimmy Carr

BUSINESS

CJ: I could practically destroy this firm if I started caring about people. I didn't get where I am today by caring about people.

The Fall and Rise Of Reginald Perrin

There's no business like showbusiness, but there are several businesses like accounting.

David Letterman

CALIFORNIA

California is a fine place to live – if you happen to be an orange.

Fred Allen

You haven't lived until you've died in California.

Mort Sahl

CAMPING

Swiss Toni: Putting up a tent is very much like making love to a beautiful woman: unzip the door, put up your pole, and slip into the old bag.

The Fast Show

CANADA

Canada is like a loft apartment over a really great party.

Robin Williams

CANDLES

Ronnie Barker (as a customer in a hardware shop): Four candles!
Ronnie Corbett (as the shop-owner): Four candles?
Ronnie Barker: Four candles.
(Ronnie Corbett gets a box down and counts out four candles on the counter.)
Ronnie Barker: No – four candles!
Ronnie Corbett: Well, there you are: four candles!
Ronnie Barker: No – fork 'andles! 'Andles for forks!

The Two Ronnies

I wanted to buy a candleholder, but the store didn't have one. So I got a cake.

Mitch Hedberg

Now, you know those trick candles that you blow out and a couple of seconds later they come alight again? Well, the other day there was a fire at the factory that makes them.

Tim Vine

Seagoon: We tried using a candle, but it wasn't very bright and we daren't light it.

The Goon Show

CAR RENTAL

I have a rented car, which is a flat-rate 12 cents a mile. In an effort to cut down on the mileage charge, I back up every place.

Woody Allen

I rent a lot of cars, but I don't always know everything about them, so a lot of times I drive for, like, ten miles with the emergency brake on. That doesn't say a lot for me, but it really doesn't say a lot for the emergency brake. It's really not an emergency brake; it's an emergency 'make the car smell funny' lever.

Mitch Hedberg

CARS

Alvy Singer (after Annie parks her car): Don't worry. We can walk to the curb from here.

Annie Hall

And we'll be talking to a car designer who's crossed Toyota with Quasimodo and come up with the Hatchback of Notre Dame.

The Two Ronnies

I don't worry about money. My wife wanted a foreign convertible. I got her one – a rickshaw.

Robert Orben

Is it just me, or does anyone else get the amount you're allowed to drink when you're driving mixed up with the amount you're allowed to take through Customs?

Harry Hill

One time a cop pulled me over for running a stop sign. He said, "Didn't you see the stop sign?" I said, "Yeah, but I don't believe everything I read."

Steven Wright

CAR BOOT SALES

Have you heard about the Irishman who reversed into a car boot sale and sold the engine?

Frank Carson

CASTLES

All castles had one major weakness: the enemy used to get in through the gift shop.

Bill Bailey

CASTRATION

Fielding: You don't have hostility to the male sex, do you?
Nancy: Oh, Women's Rights do not automatically mean castration.
Fielding: Oooh, don't say that word! Now I've got to walk around like this for two days!

Bananas

CATS

If you're sick of being covered in cat hair, get some sticky tape and wrap it around your cat.

Adam Bloom

I gave my cat a bath the other day. He just sat there. Actually, I think he enjoyed it. It wasn't very fun for me, though. The fur kind of stuck to my tongue.

Steve Martin

Mrs Premise: I just spent four hours burying the cat.

Mrs Conclusion: Four hours to bury a cat?

Mrs Premise: Yes. It wouldn't keep still: wriggling about, howling.

Monty Python's Flying Circus

The problem with cats is that they get the same exact look whether they see a moth or an axe-murderer.

Paula Poundstone

There's more than one way to skin a cat, but from the cat's perspective they all suck.

Ze Frank

They've started giving passports to animals now. My cat has a passport. Do you know how that makes Mohammed al Fayed feel?

Jeff Green

About three weeks ago I met a girl and she was real nice and she invited me to her apartment. So I went over there and she had the best pussy I have ever seen… (Audience reacts to the word "pussy".) Oh, come on! I'm talking about her cat! Now that makes me sick! You can't say anything any more that people don't take it dirty… and that disgusts me…. That cat was the best fuck I ever had.

Steve Martin

CELEBRITIES

If God doesn't destroy Hollywood Boulevard, he owes Sodom and Gomorrah an apology.

Jay Leno

LA is so celebrity-conscious, there's a restaurant that only serves Jack Nicholson… and when he shows up, they tell him there'll be a ten-minute wait.

Bill Maher

A celebrity is a person who works hard all his life to become well known, then wears dark glasses to avoid being recognized.

Fred Allen

Yeah, I love being famous. It's almost like being white, y'know?

Chris Rock

I want to be so famous that drag queens will dress like me in parades when I'm dead.

Laura Kightlinger

CENSORSHIP

Stephen: The reason we're not going to do this sketch is that it contains a great
deal of sex and violence…
Hugh: …During the sketch, Stephen hits me several times with a golf club.
Stephen: Which, of course, wouldn't matter except that I hit Hugh very sexily…
and then the sketch ends with us going to bed together.
Hugh: Violently.

A Bit Of Fry and Laurie

CHANGE

I put a dollar in a change machine. Nothing changed.

George Carlin

CHARITY

Victor: Where's that Christian Aid envelope? I'll see if I can stuff five loaves and
two pilchards into it.

One Foot In the Grave

If you take all the money we in the West spend on food in a day, it would feed the
Third World for a year. I can't help feeling we're being overcharged for our groceries.

Jimmy Carr

The Red Cross asked me for £15.62. They said it would buy five blood bags in
the Sudan. It doesn't even divide by five.

Alan Davies

No wonder Bob Geldof is such an expert on famine. He's been feeding off
'I Don't Like Mondays' for 30 years.

Russell Brand

Ted: What was it Father Jack used to say about the needy? He had a term
     for them...
Dougal: A shower of bastards.

Father Ted

This year our Help a London Junkie appeal aims to supply a million pounds'-
worth of hard drugs to the needy.

Radio Active

I saw a charity appeal in the Guardian the other day, and it read, "Little Zuki has
to walk 13 miles a day just to fetch water." And I couldn't help thinking, "She
should move."

Jimmy Carr

CHEATING

I was thrown out of NYU my freshman year. I cheated on my metaphysics final in
college. I looked within the soul of the boy sitting next to me.

Woody Allen

After being found guilty of helping Major Ingram cheat on Who Wants To Be A
Millionaire, Tecwen Whittock was threatened with prison, where he'd have no
doubt discovered a different meaning to the expression 'Fastest Finger First'.

Have I Got News For You

Fletcher: I haven't been so put out since my son Raymond crept back
     into school one night and had a prior peek at the exam papers.
Godber: Did he?
Fletcher: Yes, he did! And he still didn't bleedin' pass!

Porridge

CHEESE

Alexei Sayle (as John Cleese): Excuse me, is this a cheese shop?
Rik Mayall (as Michael Palin): Errrr, no, sir!
Sayle: Well, that's that sketch knackered then, innit?

The Young Ones

> Man (at the back of the crowd trying to hear what Jesus is saying in the
> Sermon on the Mount): I think it was, "Blessed are the cheesemakers!"
> Gregory's wife: What's so special about the cheesemakers?
> Gregory: Well, obviously it's not meant to be taken literally. It refers to any
> manufacturers of dairy products.

Monty Python's Life of Brian

CHEMICAL TOILETS

This chemical toilet is a Saniflow 33. Now, this little babe can cope with
anything, and I mean anything. Earlier on I put in a pound of mashed-up Dundee
cake. Let's take a look... not a trace! Peace of mind, I'm sure, especially if you
have elderly relatives on board.

I'm Alan Partridge

CHICAGO

I think that's how Chicago got started. A bunch of people in New York said,
"Gee, I'm enjoying the crime and the poverty, but it just isn't cold enough. Let's
go west."

Richard Jeni

CHILD BIRTH

(On whether men can appreciate the pain of childbirth): Unless you're passing
a bowling ball, I don't think so. Unless you're trying to circumsize yourself with
a chainsaw, I don't think so. Unless you're opening an umbrella up your ass, I
don't think so!

Robin Williams

Carole Burnett described what labour pains feel like. She said: "Take your
bottom lip and pull it over your head."

Bill Cosby

Coach: Norm, how come you and Vera never had any kids?
Norm: I can't, Coach.
Coach: Gee, I'm sorry, Norm.
Norm: I look at Vera – I just can't.

Cheers

Congratulations are in order for Woody Allen. He and Soon Yi have a brand-new baby daughter. It's all part of Woody's plan to grow his own wives.

David Letterman

Eddie: Oh, darling, Mummy loves you. On the day you were born I knew I
    wanted you...
Patsy: However, the next day...

Absolutely Fabulous

For a father, a home birth is preferable. That way, you're not missing anything on television.

Jeremy Hardy

I was born nine months premature.

Jay London

I was so ugly when I was born the doctor slapped my mother.

Henny Youngman

My wife: she's a beautiful woman, but in labour she turned into Jack Nicholson from The Shining. "You – you fucking did this to me!" "But I thought it was a shared experience." "No. You fucking did this!"

Lee Evans

Patsy: My mother never gave birth... she had something... removed!

Absolutely Fabulous

She didn't know what sort of birth to have, because she's quite frightened of pain. In fact, she had an epidural before they had sex.

Victoria Wood: As Seen On TV

The other day in Kentucky, a woman gave birth to a 14-pound baby boy. The baby's doing fine, but the mother is still screaming.

Conan O'Brien

She had post-natal depression. She showed me the baby… and then I had it as well.

Victoria Wood: As Seen On TV

They say men can never experience the pain of childbirth. They can… if you hit them in the goolies with a cricket bat for 14 hours.

Jo Brand

CHILDREN AND CHILDHOOD

A tip to all new mothers: don't put your baby in bed with you, because you might fall asleep, roll on it and put your back out.

Harry Hill

George: Gracie, did the maid ever drop you on your head when you were a baby?
Gracie: Don't be silly, George, we couldn't afford a maid. My mother had to do it.

George Burns and Gracie Allen

I married your mother because I wanted children. Imagine my disappointment when you came along

Groucho Marx

Social worker: Vicky, where's the baby?
Vicky Pollard: Swapped it for a Westlife CD.
Social worker: How could you do such a thing?
Vicky: I know. They're rubbish.

Little Britain

Dan: So you want to just take off and leave the kids?
Roseanne: Yes, Dan, that's all I've ever wanted!

Roseanne

Do your kids a favour – don't have any.

Robert Orben

Kids. They're not easy. But there has to be some penalty for sex.

Bill Maher

I had a traumatic childhood. I was breast-fed from falsies.

Woody Allen

I had a miserable childhood. I was in a gang called the Secret Seven and I didn't know who the other six were.

John Dowie

I had a rough childhood. You probably all know I had to escape from Nazi Germany in 1937. Well, we were living in Munich. My father was the Liberal Party candidate for Bavaria.

Eddie Izzard

Always end the name of your child with a vowel, so that when you yell, the name will carry.

Bill Cosby

Human beings are the only creatures that allow their children to come back home.

Bill Cosby

I take a very practical view of raising children. I put a sign in each of their rooms: 'Checkout time is 18 years.'

Erma Bombeck

I hurt my back the other day. I was playing piggy-back with my six-year-old nephew, and I fell off.

Tommy Cooper

I like children – properly cooked.

W C Fields

I'm actually one of six kids: Catholic. You ever notice people from big Catholic families, they always throw in that "Catholic" after the number? "Six kids: Catholic. Six kids: Catholic." Like if you didn't hear the "Catholic" part, you'd think, "Six kids? His mother really likes sex – oh, she's Catholic."

Jim Gaffigan

I'm so ugly, as a kid, I once stuck my head out the window and got arrested for mooning.

Rodney Dangerfield

It goes without saying that you should never have more children than you have car windows.

Erma Bombeck

John: Am I right in thinking that you have a daughter?
Peter: Yup. Henrietta.
John: Did he? Did he really? That must have hurt, hurt like hell.

A Bit of Fry and Laurie

Men name their children after themselves; women don't. Have you ever met a Sally Junior?

Rita Rudner

My mother loved children; she would have given anything if I'd been one.

Groucho Marx

People always ask me, "Were you funny as a child?" Well, no; I was an accountant.

Ellen DeGeneres

Roseanne: That isn't funny, Darlene. You're grounded 'til menopause!
Darlene: Yours or mine?
Roseanne: Your father's!

Roseanne

Seagoon: Listen, Auntie Min and Uncle Hen. I know you love children, but isn't it time I was weaned?
Henry: Listen, Min, he's trying to talk!

The Goon Show

When I was a kid, I asked my mother for a bubble bath, so she brought the water to a boil.

Rodney Dangerfield

Roseanne: The only thing I've ever wanted for my kids is that they're happy... and that they're out of the house, and I tell you something, happy ain't that important.

Roseanne

When my husband comes home, if the kids are still alive, I figure I've done my job.

Roseanne

Alan (to a precocious child's father): John, John, do you ever sit alone at night by the fire, with your head in your hands, and think to yourself, "God have mercy on my soul, I have spawned a monster!"

Knowing Me, Knowing You

CHILDREN'S BOOKS

Every book is a children's book if the kid can read.

Mitch Hedberg

CHINA

Apparently, one in five people in the world are Chinese. And there are five people in my family, so it must be one of them. It's either my mum or my dad. Or my older brother Colin. Or my younger brother Ho-Chan-Chu. But I think it's Colin.

Tim Vine

China has a population of a billion people. One billion. That means even if you're a one in a million kind of guy, there are still a thousand others exactly like you.

A Whitney Brown

I'll tell you what I like about Chinese people: they're hanging in there with those chopsticks. They've seen the fork, and the spoon. I don't know how they missed it. Chinese farmer, getting up, working in the field with a shovel all day. Hello... shovel! There it is! You're not plowing 40 acres with a couple of pool cues.

Jerry Seinfeld

The Chinese just put a man in space. They didn't use a rocket. They stood on each other's shoulders and passed him up.

Al Murray (The Pub Landlord)

We inadvertently bombed the Chinese Embassy, but Clinton now is working very hard. He has sent a letter of apology to the Chinese, and he's also given them a gift certificate for future nuclear secrets.

David Letterman

CHOLESTEROL

Doctor: I've got your results back from the lab, and you have the highest level of cholesterol they've ever seen. I know this is premature, but when you die, would you consider leaving your body to me?
Man: For research purposes?
Doctor: No, I want to hang you in the garden so the bluetits can peck at you.

Not the Nine O'Clock News

(Following use of the Infinite Improbability Drive) two hundred and thirty-nine thousand lightly fried eggs materialised in a large wobbly heap on the famine-struck land of Poghril. The whole Poghril tribe had died out from famine, except for one last man who died of cholesterol poisoning some weeks later.

The Hitchhiker's Guide To the Galaxy

CHRISTMAS

A severed foot is the ultimate stocking-stuffer.

Mitch Hedberg

I come from a very traditional family. When I was seven, my Uncle Terry hanged himself on Christmas Eve. My family didn't take his body down until the sixth of January.

Nick Doody

My mother-in-law has come round to our house at Christmas seven years running. This year we're having a change. We're going to let her in.

Les Dawson

Rich Hall: The nativity story in the Bible... probably they couldn't find a hotel room because they hadn't booked in advance.

Alan Davies: They should have known it would be busy 'cos it's Christmas.

QI

Santa Claus has the right idea: visit people only once a year.

Victor Borge

The TV newspeople keep saying this could be the greatest Christmas we ever had. I kind of thought the first one was.

Milton Berle

They were going to get me to turn the lights on in Belfast last Christmas. Then they changed their minds at the last minute because when the last person called Paddy was asked to press a button in Belfast, the whole of Bedford Street went up.

Patrick Kielty

CIVIL SERVANTS

Sir Humphrey: I am the Permanent Under-Secretary of State, known as the Permanent Secretary. Woolley here is your Principal Private Secretary. I too have a Principal Private Secretary and he is the Principal Private Secretary to the Permanent Secretary. Directly responsible to me are ten Deputy Secretaries, 87 Under-Secretaries and 219 Assistant Secretaries. Directly responsible to the Principal Private Secretaries are plain Private Secretaries, and the Prime Minister will be appointing two Parliamentary Under-Secretaries and you will be appointing your own Parliamentary Private Secretary.

Jim Hacker: Can they all type?

Sir Humphrey: None of us can type, Minister. Mrs Mackay types. She's the secretary.

Yes, Minister

CLASS

Jonathan Miller and myself come from good families and have had the benefit of a public school education, whereas the other two members of the cast have worked their way up from working-class origins. And yet Jonathan and I are working together with them in the cast and treating them as equals.

Peter Cook (Beyond the Fringe)

John Cleese (representing the upper class): I look down on him, because I am upper-class.
Ronnie Barker (representing the middle class): I look up to him, because he is upper-class, but I look down on him because he is lower-class. I am middle-class…
Ronnie Corbett (representing the lower class): I know my place…

The Frost Report

Mainwaring: You both went to public school, didn't you?
Wilson: You know, Sir, I can't help feeling that you've got a bit of a chip on your shoulder about that.
Mainwaring: There's no chip on my shoulder. I'll tell you what there is, though: three pips, and don't you forget it.

Dad's Army

Rich kids and poor kids are alike. They both go round huge estates with guns, out of their minds on drugs.

Jeremy Hardy

When you go to work, if your name is on the building, you're rich. If your name is on your desk, you're middle-class, and if your name is on your shirt, you're poor.

Rich Hall

I'm middle class but I'm hard. Al dente, you might say.

Jimmy Carr

CLEANLINESS

Bloodnok: You can't come in. I'm in the bath.
Seagoon: What are you doing in the bath?
Bloodnok: I'm watching television.
Seagoon: What's showing?
Bloodnok: My dear fellow: nothing. I've got a towel round me.

The Goon Show

Basil: There is your bath.
Mrs Richards: You call that a bath? It's not big enough to drown a mouse. It's disgraceful.
Basil: I wish you were a mouse…

Fawlty Towers

You know it's time to do the laundry when you dry off with a sneaker.

Zach Galifianakis

What about that advert where the guy's got blood, egg and sweat on his shirt? What did he do? Beat up a chicken?

Kit Hollerbach

I would imagine the inside of a bottle of cleaning fluid is really clean. I would imagine a vodka bottle is really drunk.

Mitch Hedberg

CLEAR OUT

There's a TV show called Clean Sweep where these women invade your home and make you throw away what you don't need. Their motto is, "If you haven't used it in six months, throw it out." By that logic, I have three weeks to get laid. And they said I couldn't write an interior decorating dick joke.

Basil White

I was cleaning out the attic the other day with the wife. Filthy, dirty and covered with cobwebs – but she's good with the kids…

Tommy Cooper

CLERGY

Ted: Dougal, how did you get into the church in the first place? Was it, like, "Collect 12 crisp packets and become a priest?"

Father Ted

David Horton: Owen, this is our new vicar.
Owen: No, it isn't! She's a woman!
Geraldine: Oh, you noticed? (Points to breasts) These are such a giveaway, aren't they?!

The Vicar of Dibley

I think priests should be allowed to get married. I think if a priest meets another priest and they like one another, they should be allowed...

Dave Allen

I would become a priest or a rabbi or a monk or whatever the hell was necessary to perform miracles such as taking money from someone else's pocket and putting it into mine, still remaining within the confines of the law.

Lenny Bruce

I'm sueing my priest, not because he molested me but because he didn't. Everyone else in the class was. What am I? Ugly or something?

James O'Loghlin

Some of my best friends are priests. Mind you, I wouldn't let my daughter marry one of them.

Dave Allen

Ted: What was that sermon about?
Dougal: Sorry, Ted, I was concentrating too hard on looking holy.

Father Ted

CLICHES

It is a cliché that most clichés are true. But then, like most clichés, that cliché is untrue.

Stephen Fry

CLOTHES

Enid: Did you get that skirt from a catalogue?
Philippa: No!
Enid: Pity. You could have sent it back.

Dinnerladies

Ali G: Respecting what you is wearing now. You is styling it, you is rocking.
     What is it?
Thomas: It's mohair.
Ali G: Mo' hair? Mo' hair, from the muff?

Ali G

Bloodnok: Now, this uniform goes back to Moss Brothers tomorrow.
Singhiz Thing: Yes, sir, there's a deposit on it.
Bloodnok: Oh, that'll brush off, don't worry.

The Last Goon Show of All

Even their clothes intimidate me. Her T-shirt said, "Mongoloid Porn Inferno". And all I could think was, "That sounds like such a busy evening."

Dylan Moran

I can remember when pants were pants. You wore them for 20 years, then you cut them down for pan scrubs.

Victoria Wood: As Seen On TV

I hate turtlenecks. Wearing a turtleneck is like being strangled by a really weak guy – all day. Like, if you wear a turtleneck and a backpack, it's like a weak midget trying to bring you down.

Mitch Hedberg

I think eventually fashion won't exist. I think some day we'll all wear the same thing, because any time I see a movie or a TV show where there are people from the future or another planet, they're all wearing the same outfit.

Jerry Seinfeld

I think that when you get dressed in the morning, sometimes you're really making a decision about your behaviour for the day. Like if you put on flip-flops, you're saying, "Hope I don't get chased today. Be nice to people in sneakers."

Demetri Martin

If women dressed for men, the stores wouldn't sell much: just an occasional sun visor.

Groucho Marx

I'm trying to think of a word to describe your outfit… "Affordable".

Dame Edna Everage

Lou: If you see a pair of pants go flyin' through the air, don't grab 'em.
Bud: Why not?
Lou: I'll be in 'em!

Abbott and Costello

Peggy Hawkins (looking at her new fur coat): Oh, Charlie! Oh, it's lovely!
Charlie Hawkins: I'll say it is. Genuine mammoth, that is.
Peggy: Oh, don't be silly, Charlie.
Charlie: Straight up. It said so on the shop window: "Mammoth fur sale."

Carry On Cabby

Trying on pants is one of the most humiliating things a man can suffer that doesn't involve a woman.

Larry David

West Mersea police announced tonight that they wished to interview a man wearing high heels and frilly knickers, but the Chief Constable said they must wear their normal uniforms.

The Two Ronnies

When you buy a V-neck sweater there's a V of material missing. You know what they do with that? They send it to Ann Summers and she makes those fancy pants.

Harry Hill

Whenever I wear something expensive, it looks stolen.

Billy Connolly

You can say what you like about long dresses, but they cover a multitude of shins.

Mae West

She said, "You're wearing two different-colored socks." I said, "I know, but to me they're the same, because I go by thickness."

Steven Wright

When a woman tries on clothing from her closet that feels tight, she'll assume she's gained weight. When a man tries something from his closet that feels tight, he'll assume the clothing has shrunk.

Rita Rudner

CLUBS

I don't care to belong to a club that accepts people like me as members.

Groucho Marx

If the bouncer gets drunk, who throws him out?

George Carlin

COFFEE

Blackadder: For the past 13 months, Baldrick's coffee has in fact been made from mud, with dandruff as a cunning sugar substitute. Just don't ask what he's been using for the milk.

Blackadder

Swiss Toni: You have to remember, Paul, that making coffee is very much like making love to a beautiful woman. It has to be hot, it has to be strong, you've got to grind your beans slowly... and at the last moment, add the milk.

The Fast Show

COLOUR SCHEMES

Thelm: That's the blue of our Margaret's shower curtain.
Pat: Where?
Thelm: Them varicose veins, there.

Victoria Wood: As Seen On TV

THE COMMON TOUCH

Mrs Merton (to Barbara Windsor): That's what I love about you, Barbara; you're one of us. You're like a big film star, but you're still common as muck!

Mrs Merton

COMMUNICATION

I feel that if a person has problems communicating, the very least he can do is to shut up.

Tom Lehrer

COMPLAINTS

Groucho: Are you the floorwalker of this ship? I want to register a complaint.
Captain Corcoran: Why? What's the matter?
Groucho: Matter enough. You know who sneaked into my stateroom at three o'clock this morning?
Captain Corcoran: Who did that?
Groucho: Nobody, and that's my complaint.

The Marx Brothers (Monkey Business)

COMPUTERS

Computer games don't affect kids. I mean, if Pac-Man affected us as kids, we'd all be running around in darkened rooms, munching magic pills and listening to repetitive music.

Marcus Brigstocke

Samantha tells me she's had to nip out to meet a nice chap who's training her in computer skills. Tonight she hopes he's going to show her the 3½-inch floppy he's got in his Mac.

I'm Sorry I Haven't A Clue

They've finally come up with the perfect office computer. If it makes a mistake, it blames another computer.

Milton Berle

Oh, so they have the internet on computers now!

Homer Simpson

A million monkeys were given a million typewriters. It's called the internet.

Simon Munnery

CONFIDENCE

Men are self-confident because they grow up identifying with superheroes. Women have bad self-images because they grow up identifying with Barbie.

Rita Rudner

Ted: The way I feel now I could convert gays!

Father Ted

CONJUGAL VISITS

Mr Barrowclough (discussing conjugal visits): I'm not aware of any prison that does that!

Fletcher: Well, maybe not here, but certainly in Holland, and also in America, I believe, where they have a more enlightened penal system anyway. They have these special apartments, where the wife comes to stay and they can manifest their long-felt want for each other.

Mr Barrowclough: You mean they spend the entire time...?

Fletcher: Conjugating, yeah.

Mr Barrowclough: That's more than I'm allowed at home!

Porridge

CONSCIENCE

Sir Humphrey: It's up to you, Bernard. What do you want?
Bernard: I want to have a clear conscience.
Sir Humphrey: When did you acquire this taste for luxuries?

Yes, Minister

CONTORTIONISM

On a packed show tonight, we'll be talking to an out-of-work contortionist who can no longer make ends meet.

The Two Ronnies

CONTRACEPTION

A new musical condom has been invented which, if it bursts, warns you to withdraw by playing Beethoven's Fifth – although Schubert's Unfinished would seem more appropriate.

Have I Got News For You

When my old man wanted sex, my mother would show him a picture of me.

Rodney Dangerfield

Condoms are useless and ineffective and they burst, and your stomach just can't cope with the sudden impact of two kilos of cocaine.

Ardal O'Hanlon

George: Why do they make the condom packets so hard to open?
Jerry: Probably to give the woman a chance to change her mind.

Seinfeld

My best birth control now is just to leave the lights on.

Joan Rivers

CONVENTION

Margaret Dumont: You must leave my room. We must have regard for certain conventions.

Groucho: One guy isn't enough; she's gotta have a convention.

The Marx Brothers (The Cocoanuts)

COSMETIC SURGERY

A woman went to a plastic surgeon and asked him to make her like Bo Derek.
He gave her a lobotomy.

Joan Rivers

I lent a friend of mine ten thousand dollars for plastic surgery, and now I don't
know what he looks like.

Emo Philips

I wish I had a twin, so I could know what I'd look like without plastic surgery.

Joan Rivers

My wife asked for plastic surgery. I cut up her credit cards.

Rodney Dangerfield

Saffy: What's Patsy having? It must be difficult to find a priority on a face like that!

Absolutely Fabulous

She got her looks from her father; he's a plastic surgeon.

Groucho Marx

She probably used some expensive monkey-gland preparation for the
purpose of preservation, and it certainly served its function: all of her
wrinkles were well preserved.

Lenny Bruce

There's so much Botox around now that you can't tell when a Jewish girl is angry!

Mort Sahl

COUNTING

King Arthur: One, two… five!
Sir Galahad: Three, sire!
King Arthur: THREE!

Monty Python and the Holy Grail

Alan Davies: How many grains of sand in the Sahara, then, do you reckon?
Stephen Fry: I lost count. It's quite a few. I got up to 17 and it's definitely more
than that.

QI

CRABS

Patrick (explaining where he's been since a crab crawled out of Victor
Meldrew's garden and up his shorts): Just up the hospital to have a hermit crab
surgically removed from my testicles. It wasn't demonstrating much in the way
of hermitude when it popped into my shorts earlier on for lunch and fastened
itself to my scrotum like a bulldog clip. I completely forgot to smear my groin
with crab repellent.

One Foot In the Grave

CREATIONISM

You ever noticed how people who believe in creationism look really unevolved?

Bill Hicks

"God put them (dinosaur fossils) here to test our faith!" I think God put you here
to test my faith, dude.

Bill Hicks

CRIME

Mugger: Your money or your life! Come on! Your money or your life!
Jack Benny: I'm thinking about it!

Jack Benny

Godber: I'm only in here due to tragic circumstances.
Fletcher: Which were?
Godber: I got caught.

Porridge

Bilko: There's no stealing in the army: just a lot of equipment keeps
moving around.

The Phil Silvers Show

A recent police study found that you're much more likely to get shot by a fat cop if you run.

Dennis Miller

Are you going to come quietly, or do I have to use earplugs?

Spike Milligan

People knock ASBOs, but you have to bear in mind they're the only qualification some of these kids are going to get.

Linda Smith

Sir Arthur (discussing the Great Train Robbery): I'd like to make one thing quite clear at the outset: when you speak of a train robbery, this in fact involved no loss of train. They're very hard to lose, you see, being so bulky.

Beyond the Fringe

If you ever see me being beaten up by the cops, put down the video camera and come help me, all right?

Bobcat Goldthwait

Seagoon: What did this attacker look like?
Willium: I dunno. I dunno. I didn't see him, mate.
Seagoon: I see, and would you recognise him if you didn't see him again?
Willium: Straightaway!

The Goon Show

Kryten: This man is not guilty of manslaughter. He's only guilty of being Arnold J. Rimmer. That is his crime. It is also his punishment.

Red Dwarf

Mackay: All right, Fletcher, just don't let me catch you thieving!
Fletcher: I won't, Mr Mackay.
Mackay: You won't what?
Fletcher: I won't let you catch me, Mr Mackay!

Porridge

A cement mixer has collided with a prison van on the Kingston by-pass. Motorists are asked to be on the lookout for 16 hardened criminals.

The Two Ronnies

Someone stole all my credit cards, but I won't be reporting it. The thief spends less than my wife did.

Henny Youngman

What's the difference between a pickpocket and a peeping tom? A pickpocket snatches watches.

Redd Foxx

Chisholm: The black-bearded criminal must have got in through the door or the windows. Everything else was locked.

The Goon Show

What a detective! Once a burglar robbed a safe wearing calfskin gloves. He took the fingerprints and five days later he arrested a cow in Surrey.

Morecambe and Wise

CRUCIFIXION

A lot of Christians wear crosses around their necks. You think when Jesus comes back, he ever wants to see a fucking cross? Kind of like going up to Jackie Onassis with a rifle pendant on, you know? "Just thinking of John, Jackie. Just thinking of John. Just thinking of John, baby."

Bill Hicks

Co-ordinator: Crucifixion?
Mr Cheeky: Er, no, freedom, actually.
Co-ordinator: What?
Mr Cheeky: Yeah, they said I hadn't done anything and I could go and live on an island somewhere.
Co-ordinator: Oh, I say, that's very nice. Well, off you go then.
Mr Cheeky: No! I'm just pulling your leg! It's crucifixion really!

Monty Python's Life of Brian

CRYING

Men do cry, but only when assembling furniture from Ikea.

Rita Rudner

CUBA

A group of Cuban Americans denounced the Castro government as a fascist regime that monitors and scrutinises its citizens' everyday existence. And then they excused themselves to go watch Big Brother.

Bill Maher

My wife is teaching me Cuban. It's like Spanish, but with fewer words for luxury goods.

Emo Philips

CULTS

Dougal: God, I've heard about those cults, Ted: people dressing up in black and saying Our Lord's going to come back and save us all.
Ted: No, Dougal, that's us; that's Catholicism.
Dougal: Oh, right.

Father Ted

CUNNING PLANS

Baldrick: I have a plan, sir.
Blackadder: Really, Baldrick? A cunning and subtle one?
Baldrick: Yes, Sir.
Blackadder: As cunning as a fox who's just been appointed Professor of Cunning at Oxford University?
Baldrick: Yes, Sir.
(Whistles sound, ordering troops to prepare to go over the top.)
Blackadder: Well, I'm afraid it's too late. Whatever it was, I'm sure it was better than my plan to get out of here by pretending to be mad. I mean, who would have noticed another madman round here?

Blackadder Goes Forth

CUSTER'S LAST STAND

My wife's great-grandfather was actually killed at Custer's Last Stand. He didn't actually take part in the fighting; he was camping nearby and he went over to complain about the noise.

Ronnie Corbett

CUSTOMERS

Basil: A satisfied customer. We should have him stuffed.

Fawlty Towers

CYCLING

A vicar who rode his bicycle the wrong way up the M6 was asked in court how on earth he managed to avoid an accident. He replied, "God was with me." He was further charged with riding two up on a bike.

The Two Ronnies

Mountain bikes. What's that all about? There's no mountains in north London. If I'm going out I don't think, "Shall I cycle or take the chairlift?"

Alan Davies

DAIRY FARMING

Charlie Muggins: Hello, what's a nice girl like you doing with an old cow?
Girl with cow: I'm taking her to the bull.
Muggins: Well, couldn't your father do that?
Girl: No, it must be the bull.

Carry On Camping

DANCING

Firefly: I could dance with you until the cows come home. On second thoughts, I'd rather dance with the cows until you come home.

The Marx Brothers (Duck Soup)

I grew up with six brothers. That's how I learned to dance: waiting for the bathroom.

Bob Hope

Remember those magical nights, Cynthia? We'd dance cheek to cheek. I'd rub my stubble against yours.

Milton Berle

DANGER

Danger could be my middle name… but it's John.

Eddie Izzard

DARKNESS

As is traditional on these occasions, Samantha went along to the gramophone library earlier to collect the teams' records. It's pitch-black down there, so Samantha and the elderly archivist have taken to searching the shelves by candlelight, which can be messy, so while Samantha passes down the discs, the nice man holds the ladder while he cleans the dust and wax off in the dark.

I'm Sorry I Haven't A Clue

DATING

Elaine: So you're saying that 95 per cent of the population is undateable?
Jerry: UNDATEABLE!
Elaine: Then how are all these people getting together?
Jerry: Alcohol!

Seinfeld

A girl I was dating once told me on the phone, "Can you hold? There's a telemarketer on the other line."

Zach Galifianakis

A girl phoned me the other day and said, "Come on over; there's nobody home." I went over. Nobody was home.

Rodney Dangerfield

A woman broke up with me and sent me pictures of her and her new boyfriend in bed together. Solution? I sent them to her dad.

Christopher Case

He spiked my drink with speed. I didn't mind so much. I got loads of hoovering done.

Sarah Millican

Allan: What are you doing Saturday night?
Intense girl in museum: Committing suicide.
Allan: What about Friday night?

Play It Again, Sam

Elaine: You know what your problem is? Your standards are too high.
Jerry: I went out with you.
Elaine: That's because my standards are too low.

Seinfeld

I've been on so many blind dates, I should get a free dog.

Wendy Liebman

Jeff: Rule one of playing it cool: only smile at her face.

Coupling

Men don't realise that if we're sleeping with them on the first date, we're
probably not interested in seeing them again either.

Chelsea Handler

DEAFNESS

You can say what you like about deaf people...

Jimmy Carr

I wonder if deaf people have a sign for "Talk to the hand"?

Zach Galifianakis

I had a job selling hearing aids door to door. It wasn't easy, because your best
prospects never answered.

Bob Monkhouse

DEATH

Bob: Emily, aren't you afraid of death?
Emily: I just think of it as a part of life.
Bob: Yeah, the last part.

The Bob Newhart Show

Blanche: Drink and sex. That's what killed your uncle: drink and sex!

Harry: Yeah. He couldn't get either, so he shot himself.

The Benny Hill Show

Boris: Death should not be seen as the end, but as a very effective way to cut down expenses.

Love and Death

Charlie Roper (to the patient in the hospital bed next to him): Last bloke in that bed had the same thing.

Francis Bigger: Did he?

Charlie: Right up to the end.

Bigger: Well that's cheerful. I'll say one thing for them: it's a nice warm bed.

Charlie: Should be, they only took him out half an hour ago.

Carry On Doctor

Dorothy (to Blanche): How long did you wait to have sex after George died?

Sophia: 'Til the paramedics came.

The Golden Girls

Dreyfus: I wish you were DEAD!

Clouseau: Well, of course, you are entitled to your opinion.

Return of the Pink Panther

I know when I'm going to die; my birth certificate has an expiration date.

Steven Wright

I want to die before my wife, and the reason is this: is it's true that when you die, your soul goes up to judgment, I don't want my wife up there ahead of me to tell them things.

Bill Cosby

I'm not afraid to die. I just don't want to be there when it happens.

Woody Allen

Dying can damage your health. Every coffin contains a Government Health Warning.

Spike Milligan

(Checking patient's pulse) Either he's dead or my watch has stopped.

Groucho Marx

For three days after death hair and fingernails continue to grow, but phone calls taper off.

Johnny Carson

I always remember the last words of my grandfather: "A truck!"

Emo Philips

My father died while he was fucking. He came and went at the same time.

Richard Pryor

If you really believe that death leads to eternal bliss, then why are you wearing a seatbelt?

Doug Stanhope

Journalist (visiting a woman whose husband has died recently): Good excuse, a death, isn't it, to bunk off the housework? If somebody dropped dead in our house, I'd be quite pleased.
Widow: Would you like a drink?
Journalist: Depends what he died of. If it's anything catching, I won't bother, ta.

Victoria Wood: As Seen On TV

I'll tell you what makes my blood boil: crematoriums.

Tim Vine

Last month, my aunt passed away. She was cremated. We think that's what did it.

Jonathan Katz

My uncle's dying wish was to have me sitting on his lap. He was in the electric chair.

Rodney Dangerfield

Boris (on being challenged to a duel to the death): I can't do anything to the death: doctor's orders. I have an ulcer and dying is one of the worst things for it.

Love and Death

DEFENCE

Tom: We spend over 50 billion dollars a year on defence. We don't need more allies.
Dick: Well, what do we need?
Tom: We need... more enemies.

The Smothers Brothers

DEMOCRACY

Listening to the voice of the people... I don't want to trust the judgment of any group of people that can put Bryan Adams at number one for 15 weeks.

Frank Skinner

DEMOLITION

Frankie Boyle (asked to come up with 'bad things to say at the opening of the new Wembley Stadium'): Cost a hundred million pounds to demolish Wembley. If you'd had your last game against Scotland, we'd have done it for nothing!

Mock the Week

DENTAL WORK

All dentists are people who got into medical school and decided after two weeks they're way out of their depth and think: "I'm leaving. I'll just take the page on teeth, if you don't mind."

Jack Dee

I had to have a brace because I had big teeth. If I'd gone to Africa, I'd have got poached.

Alan Carr

I swear, if Colgate comes out with one more type of toothpaste... I just want clean teeth; that's all I want. I don't want the tartar and I don't want the cavities. And I want white teeth. How come I have to choose? And then they have the 'Colgate Total' that supposedly has everything in there. I don't believe that for one second. If it's all in the one, how come they make all the others? Who's going: "I don't mind the tartar so much?"

Ellen DeGeneres

DEPRESSION

Basil: Manuel, my wife informs me that you're... depressed. Let me tell you
     something. Depression is a very bad thing. It's like a virus. If you don't stamp
     on it, it spreads throughout the mind, and then one day you wake up in the
     morning and you... you can't face life any more!
Sybil: And then you open a hotel.

Fawlty Towers

We had a depression fair in the back yard. A major game there was Pin the
Blame On the Donkey.

Richard Lewis

DESERT ISLAND DISCS

I was on Desert Island Discs with Sue Lawley. She asked me for two books
I'd take with me to a desert island, and I didn't like the threat implied in that
question. I said that the first would be a big, inflatable book, and the second
would be How to Make Oars Out Of Sand.

Ardal O'Hanlon

DETERMINATION

There comes a time in the affairs of man when he must take the bull by the tail
and face the situation.

W C Fields

DETERRING BREAK IN

You break into my house, I will shoot you. My wife will shoot you and then spend
30 minutes telling you why she shot you.

Jeff Foxworthy

DEVIL WORSHIP

I'm a dyslexic Satanist. I worship the drivel.

Linda Smith

High Priest: Well, that's just great, isn't it? No virgin's blood to drink. None of you lot are virgins, I suppose? Thought not. Anyone done it… less than twenty times? Forty times?

Woman Diabolist: I don't enjoy it. Does that count?

The Million-Pound Radio Show

DICTATION

(Dictating a telegram to be sent to a lady friend) Then I want to end up, "Norwich". Yes, well, it's an epigrammatic way of saying, "Knickers off ready when I come home." It's the initial letters of each word… Yes, I know 'knickers' is spelt with a K. I did go to Oxford. It was one of the first things they taught us.

Alan Bennett (On the Margin)

DICTIONARIES

The other night I was reading the dictionary. I thought it was a poem about everything.

Steven Wright

Dr Johnson: This book, sir, contains every word in our beloved language!

Blackadder: Every single one, sir?

Dr Johnson: Every single word, sir!

Blackadder: Oh. Well, in that case, sir, I hope you will not object if I also offer the Doctor my most enthusiastic… contrafibularities.

Blackadder

DIETING

Barbara Royle: How's your diet going, Cheryl?

Cheryl: Oh, all right, thanks, yeah, Barbara. I lost four pounds… and then I put two back on and then another two. But I've not gained any.

The Royle Family

Marjorie Dawes: Dust. Anybody? No? High in fat? Low in fat? Dust. Anybody? No? Dust. Anybody? No? Dust. Anybody? No? Dust. Anybody? No? Dust. Anybody? No? Dust. It's actually very low in fat. You can have as much dust as you like.

Little Britain

Maltesers have the less fattening centre. Well, yes, but they are covered in chocolate. That's like saying: "I'll have a mineral water, please. Can you put some cubes of lard in it?"

Linda Smith

My wife's on a new diet: coconuts and bananas. She hasn't lost weight, but can she climb a tree!

Henny Youngman

I haven't got a waist. I've just got a sort of place a bit like an unmarked level crossing.

Victoria Wood: As Seen On TV

The second day of a diet is always easier than the first. By the second day, you're off it.

Jackie Gleason

You know you've been on a diet too long when cat food commercials make you hungry.

Andy Bumatai

Marjorie Dawes: Now, crisps are high in fat, but they're also low in protein and low in fibre! See? It's not all bad!

Little Britain

I've been on a constant diet for the last two decades. I've lost a total of 789 pounds. By all accounts, I should be hanging from a charm bracelet.

Erma Bombeck

DIGITAL CAMERAS

The digital camera is a great invention because it allows us to reminisce. Instantly.

Demetri Martin

DIRECTIONS

If you're in a car with a man and he stops and asks for directions, listen carefully, because he won't, and it will be your fault if you get lost.

Rita Rudner

Presenter: Good evening and welcome to Realising I've Given The Wrong Directions. Tonight I shall be realising I've given the wrong directions to Rabbi Michael Leibovitz. Sadly, Rabbi Leibovitz is unable to be with us tonight. Till next time, bye-bye.
A Bit Of Fry and Laurie

DISABILITY

There's many a pianist who would give their right arm to play like Colin Sell. In fact, losing an arm would be a very good way to perfect the technique.

I'm Sorry I Haven't A Clue

Peter (to a one-legged man auditioning for the role of Tarzan): The leg division, Mr Spiggott. You are deficient in it – to the tune of one. Your right leg I like. I like your right leg. A lovely leg for the role; that's what I said when I saw it come in. I said, "A lovely leg for the role." I've got nothing against your right leg. The trouble is, neither have you.

Peter Cook and Dudley Moore (One Leg Too Few)

What do you say to a bloke who's got no arms and no legs if your watch is broken? Have you got the time on yer, cock?

Kevin Turvey (Rik Mayall)

If this is the answer, what is the question: Up To 18 Months.
Hugh Dennis: How long does it take Abu Hamza to tie his shoelace?

Mock the Week

DISAGREEMENT

He who disagrees with me in private: call him a fool. He who disagrees with me in public: call him an ambulance.

Simon Munnery

DISEASE

Everything that used to be a sin is now a disease.

Bill Maher

Wouldn't it be great if you could only get AIDS by giving money to television preachers?

Elayne Boosler

DIVORCE

Divorce: from the Latin word meaning "to rip out a man's genitals through his wallet."

Robin Williams

It is a sad fact that 50 percent of marriages in this country end in divorce, but, hey, the other half end in death. You could be one of the lucky ones!

Richard Jeni

Allan: My parents never got divorced, although I begged them to.

Play It Again, Sam

George: Divorce is always hard, especially on the kids. 'Course, I'm the result of my parents having stayed together, so you never know.

Seinfeld

Instead of getting married again, I'm going to find a woman I don't like and give her a house.

Lewis Grizzard

My wife Mary and I have been married for 47 years and not once have we had an argument serious enough to consider divorce: murder, yes, but divorce – never.

Jack Benny

Paying alimony is like feeding hay to a dead horse.

Groucho Marx

In New York State, they have a strange law that says you can't get a divorce unless you can prove adultery, and it's weird, because the Ten Commandments say, "Thou shalt not commit adultery" – but New York State says you have to.

Woody Allen

DOGS

A dog is not intelligent. Never trust an animal that's surprised by its own farts.

Frank Skinner

A Canadian psychologist is selling a video that teaches you how to test your dog's IQ. Here's how it works: if you spend $12.99 for the video, your dog is smarter than you.

Jay Leno

I went for skill rather than looks when I got my dog. I got an ex-drug sniffer dog: comes in very useful at parties.

Sean Hughes

Martin (referring to his dog Eddie): I call him Eddie Spaghetti.
Daphne: Oh, he likes pasta?
Martin: No, he has worms.

Frasier

My wife kisses the dog on the lips, yet she won't drink from my glass!

Rodney Dangerfield

I spilled spot remover on my dog. Now he's gone.

Steven Wright

You can say any fool thing to a dog, and the dog will give you this look that says, "My God, you're RIGHT! I NEVER would've thought of that!"

Dave Barry

DOORS

You ever see that sign: "This Door Must Remain Shut At All Times"? Why have a goddamn door?

Gallagher

DOUBLE BOOKING

Frankie Boyle (asked to come up with 'bad things to say at the opening of the new Wembley Stadium'): Due to a double booking, England's first match is against Simply Red!

Mock the Week

DOUBLE MEANINGS

The marvellous thing about a joke with a double meaning is that it can only mean one thing.

Ronnie Barker

DREAMS

Biddle: Nurse, I dreamt about you last night.
Nurse Clarke: Did you?
Biddle: No, you wouldn't let me.

Carry On Doctor

DRESSING UP

My father used to like my mother to get dressed up as a nurse. Then he used to like her to go out to work... as a nurse! Brought in some extra money...

Harry Hill

DRUGS

I don't do drugs. If I want a rush I just stand up when I'm not expecting it.

Dylan Moran

Don't do drugs, kids. There's a time and place for everything. It's called college.

South Park

If they took all the drugs, nicotine, alcohol and caffeine off the market for six days, they'd have to bring out the tanks to control you.

Dick Gregory

I've had bad times on drugs too. I mean, shit, look at this haircut.

Bill Hicks

"You once said you had a drug problem…"
"Yeah, I still do. It's so hard to find good grass these days."

Lily Tomlin

Do you remember when Frank Bough used to be on that Holiday programme? He was always going to Colombia, wasn't he? Judith Chalmers used to ring him up and say, "What are you doing over there, Frank?" "I'm doing about two grands'-worth, me!"

Richard Morton

Cocaine is God's way of saying you're making too much money.

Robin Williams

I'm not addicted to cocaine… I just like the way it smells.

Richard Pryor

Marijuana? It's harmless really, unless you fashion it into a club and beat somebody over the head with it.

Bill Bailey

The best pitch I ever heard about cocaine was back in the early eighties when a street dealer followed me down the sidewalk going, "I got some great blow, man. I got the stuff that killed Belushi."

Denis Leary

Who did ITV get to present the late-night section of their all-night telethon? Frank Bough! Every day was Red Nose Day for Frank, if you know what I mean.

Richard Morton

Do you know what the good side of crack is? If you're up at the right hour, you can get a VCR for $1.50. You can furnish your whole house for $10.95.

Chris Rock

I noticed this sickly-sweet smell. I thought, "Aye aye, Spam for tea." Then I saw them: the extra-long nine-skin Gauloise dick compensators they were rolling. I said, "Byron, how did you manage to get the spam in there?"

Alexei Sayle

One time when me was high, me sold me car for like 24 Chicken McNuggets.

Ali G

I knew I had a drug problem when I got a voicemail message – from myself. "This is you. Marijuana has destroyed your short-term memory, so write this down. Buy more marijuana. Save this message."

Basil White

Marijuana will be legal some day, because the many law students who now smoke pot will some day become Congressmen and legalise it in order to protect themselves.

Lenny Bruce

The main problem with heroin is that it's very moreish.

Harry Hill

Phoebe: Look, I had a hard life. My mother was killed by a drug-dealer.
Monica: Phoebe, your mom killed herself.
Phoebe: She was a drug-dealer.

Friends

Saffy: I thought they didn't let people with drug convictions into America.
Patsy: It's not so much a conviction, darling. It's more of a strong belief.

Absolutely Fabulous

Why are there no recreational drugs taken in suppository form?

George Carlin

How about a positive LSD story? Wouldn't that be newsworthy, just the once? "Today, a young man on acid realised that all matter is merely energy condensed to a slow vibration; that we are all one consciousness experiencing itself subjectively. There is no such thing as death, life is only a dream and we're the imagination of ourselves… Here's Tom with the weather!"

Bill Hicks

DRY SKIN

And John said, "Hey, what are those white specks on your leg?" and I looked down and I had all this terrible dandruff, all round the tops of my legs – like, really obvious with my tan. And it was like, you know, bikini dandruff.

Victoria Wood: As Seen On TV

Right; dry skin cream. I'm having an attack of the old flákes again. This morning, my pillow looked like a flapjack.

I'm Alan Partridge

DUDE

I wonder what the most intelligent thing ever said was that started with the word "Dude." "Dude, these are isotopes." "Dude, we removed your kidney. You're gonna be fine." "Dude, I am so stoked to win this Nobel Prize. I just wanna thank Kevin, and Turtle, and all my homies."

Demetri Martin

DUST MITES

I'm worried about dust mites. Apparently there's a million of them in your bed eating your dead skin. How can you have a million of anything in your bed with you and not notice?

Alan Davies

DYSLEXIA

Old McDonald was dyslexic, E-O-I-O-E.

Billy Connolly

EARLY

Peter: Relax, John. It's still early.

John: I know, Peter. But it's not going to stay early for long… (Looking out of the window) There are six million people out there, Peter.

Peter: Really? What do they want?

A Bit Of Fry and Laurie

EARS

Ted: He gets a kind of waxy build-up in his ears.

Dougal: Yeah, but it's good though, in a way, 'cos we never run short of candles.

Father Ted

EATING OUT

And can I have the same, please, but with different-shaped pasta? What do you call those pasta in bows? Like a bow-tie, but miniature? Like an Action Man bow-tie?

I'm Alan Partridge

Bren: Twink, what's the soup?

Twinkle: Minestrone.

Bren: Well, why's it not on the menu?

Twinkle: Can't spell it!

Dinnerladies

I took the wife's family out for tea and biscuits. They weren't too happy about having to give blood, though.

Les Dawson

Master Heath: I don't like the chips. The chips are awful.

Basil: Really? How so?

Master Heath: They're the wrong shape and they're just awful.

Basil Fawlty: Oh, my... What shape do you prefer? Mickey Mouse-shape? Smarties-shape? Amphibious landing craft-shape? Poke-in-the-eye shape?

Fawlty Towers

There's a lot of stupid rules connected with eating out, like you should only ever drink white wine with fish. That's bloody stupid, isn't it? Have you ever tried getting pissed with a haddock?

Alexei Sayle

You know mini-kievs, yeah? On the menu, would they be under starters or main courses?... I'll get me coat.

The Fast Show

This greasy spoon restaurant was so bad, on the menu there were even flies in the pictures.

Richard Lewis

Burger giants McDonald's are opening a restaurant inside Guy's Hospital in London. Hospital chiefs presumably chose McDonald's on the basis that it's the only food that makes hospital meals seem good.

Have I Got News for You

McDonald's 'Breakfast for under a dollar' actually costs much more than that. You have to factor in the cost of coronary bypass surgery.

George Carlin

Why did Colonel Sanders keep his 11 herbs and spices a secret? Because he was ashamed of them.

Neil Hamburger

One day, I was walking into Kentucky Fried Chicken, and I ordered three buckets of chicken – 24 pieces in each bucket – and the lady asked me, "Is this here or to go?"

George Wallace

Why does KFC come in a bucket? So you have something to throw up into afterwards.

Neil Hamburger

Mrs Bun: Have you got anything without Spam in it?
Waitress: Well, there's Spam, egg, sausage and Spam. That's not got much
Spam in it.

Monty Python's Flying Circus

ECONOMIC THEORY

Fran: You know, in Tibet, if they want something, do you know what they do?
They give something away.
Bernard: Do they? Do they? That must be why they're such a dominant global power.

Black Books

EDUCATION

How is education supposed to make me feel smarter? Besides, every time I learn something new, it pushes some old stuff out of my brain. Remember when I took that home winemaking course, and I forgot how to drive?

Homer Simpson

Education isn't everything; for a start, it isn't an elephant.

Spike Milligan

Education is worth a whole lot. Just think, with enough education and brains the average man would make a good lawyer – and so would the average lawyer.

Gracie Allen

If one of the boys was considered emotionally disturbed the headmaster used to sit the lad in a chair in his study, get down his great volume entitled Child Psychology and hit him on the head with it – you could always tell the emotionally disturbed kids – they had shorter necks than the others.

Ronnie Corbett

You know there is a problem with the education system when you realize that out of the 3 R's only one begins with an R.

Dennis Miller

Blanche: [My professor] told me the only way I'd get an A on his final is
    if I sleep with him.
Rose: No!
Blanche: Yes. I don't know what I'm gonna do!
Sophia: Get it in writing!

The Golden Girls

By the time you're 80 years old you've learned everything. You only have to
remember it.

George Burns

College atheletes used to get a degree in bringing your pencil.

Ruby Wax

I know I've got a degree. Why does that mean I have to spend my life with
intellectuals? I've got a lifesaving certificate, but I don't spend my evenings diving
for a rubber brick with my pyjamas on.

Victoria Wood: As Seen On TV

I went to my English teacher and I said, "Mr Spinoza, which A-levels do you think
I should take?" and he said, "Think of the things you like doing and take subjects
involving doing those." So I'm doing eating, sleeping and wanking at A-level.

Daniel Kitson

I won't say ours was a tough school, but we had our own coroner. We used to
write essays like: What I'm going to be if I grow up.

Lenny Bruce

I'm not sure it matters what school you go to, as long as you're not stabbed.

Linda Smith

Madam, there's no such thing as a tough child. If you parboil them first for seven
hours, they always come out tender.

W C Fields

Old professors never die, they just lose their faculties.

Stephen Fry

Our bombs are smarter than the average high school student. At least they can find Kuwait.

A Whitney Brown

Roy (singing): We don't need no education.
Moss: Yes, you do; you've just used a double negative.

The IT Crowd

When I was young my parents used to say to me: "To pay for your education, your father and I had to make a lot of sacrifices." And it was true, 'cos they were both druids.

Milton Jones

ELECTRICITY

I've had all the electric leads in my house shortened to save on electricity.

Gracie Allen

ELEPHANTS

I once shot an elephant in my pyjamas. How he got into my pyjamas, I'll never know.

Groucho Marx

ELVIS

If life was fair, Elvis would be alive and all the impersonators would be dead.

Johnny Carson

EMAIL

I barely check my email any more because half of the time, it's the same ad: "Do you want bigger breasts?" and after a year or so of getting those emails… um… I'm thinking about it. Even after I'm not funny any more, people will still come to see me. "Ah, well, he's not funny, but Jesus, look at the rack on him!"

Lewis Black

EMBARRASSMEMT

Isn't it embarrassing when you cough up a hairball and it isn't your colour?

Harry Hill

EMERGENCIES

Rimmer: Step up to Red Alert!
Kryten: Sir, are you absolutely sure? It does mean changing the bulb.

Red Dwarf

Operator! Give me the number for 911!

Homer Simpson

Cat: Forget red – let's go all the way up to Brown Alert!
Kryten: There's no such thing as a Brown Alert, sir.
Cat: You won't be saying that in a minute!

Red Dwarf

ENQUIRIES

People come up to me and say: "Emo, do people really come up to you?"

Emo Philips

ENVIRONMENTAL ISSUES

That was "Big Yellow Taxi" by Joni Mitchell, a song in which Joni complains they 'paved paradise to put up a parking lot', a measure which actually would have alleviated traffic congestion on the outskirts of paradise, something which Joni singularly fails to point out, perhaps because it doesn't quite fit in with her blinkered view of the world. Nevertheless, nice song.

I'm Alan Partridge

The rain forest has Sting. Now Siberia has Jack Dee. Someone had to draw the short straw. In this case it was the rain forest.

Jack Dee

EXPERIENCE

Experience is the stuff that when you finally get enough of, you're too old to qualify for the job.

Robert Orben

EQUALITY

The man who said, "All men are created equal" has never been in a footballers' changing room.

Morecambe and Wise

ESCALATORS

If I have to move up in a building, I choose the elevator over the escalator, because one time I was riding the escalator and I tripped. I fell down the stairs for an hour and a half.

Demetri Martin

ESTATE AGENTS

Estate agents... There's only one thing worse than an estate agent, but at least that can be safely lanced, drained and surgically dressed. Estate agents. Love them or loathe them, you'd be mad not to loathe them.

Stephen Fry

When an estate agent gets mugged, do you think the police actually believe their description of what went on? "Yes, officer, I was pushed into quite a spacious alley, only two miles from the train station. I was then punched in my face, which still retains some of its original features."

Sean Meo

ETERNITY

Saw a guy with a sign that said, "Where Will You Spend Eternity?" Which freaked me out, because I was on my way to the Motor Vehicle Agency.

Arj Barker

ETIQUETTE

At a formal dinner party, the person nearest death should always be seated closest to the bathroom.

George Carlin

Ben Stiller: You wouldn't even shake my hand the first time we met...
Larry: You sneezed! You had snot all over your hand!
Stiller: That was a dry sneeze, Larry!
Larry: I can't assume dry; I gotta assume wet!

Curb Your Enthusiasm

EUPHEMISM

Vicar: As I was on my way here tonight, I arrived at the station and, by an oversight, I happened to come out by the way one is supposed to go in. And as I was coming out, an employee of the railway company hailed me. "Hey, Jack," he shouted, "where do you think you are going?" That, at any rate, was the gist of what he said.

Alan Bennett (Beyond the Fringe)

EUROPE

And where would we be without rules, eh? That's right. France. And where would we be with too many rules? Germany.

Al Murray (The Pub Landlord)

I grew up in Europe, where the history comes from.

Eddie Izzard

EVIL

When choosing between two evils, I always like to try the one I've never tried before.

Mae West

EVOLUTION

We got new advice as to what motivated man to walk upright: to free his hands for masturbation.

Jane Wagner

EXAGGERATION

There are some men so addicted to exaggeration that they can't tell the truth without lying.

Josh Billings

EXAMS

I managed to get through the mining exams. They're not very rigorous. They only ask you one question. They say, "Who are you?" And I got 75 per cent on that.

Peter Cook

EXCITEMENT

Alice: I'm so excited I could just burst, like a great big blister when you pop it with a pin!

The Vicar of Dibley

Allan: I'm so excited, I think I'll brush all my teeth today!

Play It Again, Sam

EXCUSES

Why did I sit with her? Because she reminds me of you. That's why I'm here with you. Because you remind me of you; your eyes, your throat, your lips, everything about you reminds me of you – except you. How do you account for that? If she figures that one out, she's good.

Groucho Marx

EXCUSES FOR BEING LATE

Reggie: Eleven minutes late; somebody had stolen the lines at Surbiton.

The Fall and Rise Of Reginald Perrin

Reggie: Seventeen minutes late; water seeping through the cables at Effingham Junction. There was a lot of Effingham and a good deal of Blindingham!

The Fall and Rise Of Reginald Perrin

EXERCISE

I bought a cross-trainer to keep fit. I suppose that it's not enough to just buy it.

Sarah Millican

Edina: Soon I'll be bendy like Madonna, darling. Then I'll be able to kiss my own ass from both directions.

Absolutely Fabulous

Guys, you've got to be careful of this body-building stuff because what happens is your entire body gets puffed out, but your head remains exactly the same size. And this is to say nothing of your genitals.

Kit Hollerbach

I ran three miles today. Finally, I said: "Lady, take your purse."

Emo Philips

If God had intended Jewish women to exercise, he would have put diamonds on the floor.

Joan Rivers

I'm not into working out. My philosophy is no pain, no pain.

Carol Leifer

My doctor recently told me that jogging could add years to my life. I think he was right. I feel ten years older already.

Milton Berle

My grandmother started walking five miles a day when she was 60. She's 97 now, and we don't know where the hell she is.

Ellen DeGeneres

My mother-in-law had to stop skipping for exercise. It registered seven on the Richter scale.

Les Dawson

So I said to the gym instructor: "Can you teach me to do the splits?" He said: "How flexible are you?" I said: "I can't make Tuesdays."

Tim Vine

EXPLOSIVE DEVICES

Clouseau (having just been presented at the door with a bomb): Special delivery – a beumb. Were you expecting one?

Revenge of the Pink Panther

George: If we do happen to step on a mine, Sir, what do we do?
Blackadder: Normal procedure, Lieutenant, is to jump 200 feet in the air and scatter oneself over a wide area.

Blackadder

Now, you're perfectly safe, Willard; there's nothing to worry about as long as it's ticking… Er, when it stops ticking, that's something else again, Willard.

Bob Newhart (Defusing a Bomb)

FAINT PRAISE

The producer… he's a nice man… underneath.

Frankie Howerd

Raquel: Derek, will you get it into your thick skull, I'm not trying to meet intelligent and sensitive people. I'm happy with you!

Only Fools And Horses

FAMILIES

George Burns: Are you the oldest in the family?
Gracie Allen: No, no, my mother and father are much older.

The Burns and Allen Show

Happiness is having a large, loving, caring, close-knit family – in another city.

George Burns

I came from a very big family. There were so many wet nappies in the kitchen there was a rainbow in the lobby.

Les Dawson

There is no such thing as "fun for the whole family".

Jerry Seinfeld

I know it's too late now, but I have long felt that I was foolish not to limit my family… to a parakeet with his tongue clipped.

Erma Bombeck

FARMING

Samantha tells me she has to nip off to a rare breeds farm where they still plough with huge beasts of burden. She's become friendly with a couple of farmhands who are going to show her their gigantic ox.

I'm Sorry I Haven't A Clue

FASCISTS

Ted: I'm not a fascist. I'm a priest. Fascists dress up in black and tell people what to do, whereas priests...

Father Ted

Women want men in uniforms. In fact, when you actually get down to it, all women really want are fascists. Hey, you can say what you like about the Nazis, but those guys knew how to turn heads.

Dylan Moran

FAT

A new study says that over half of all Californians are obese. In fact, half of Californians are really two-thirds of Californians.

Jay Leno

Big bottom, big bottom,
Talk about mud flaps, my girl's got 'em!

Spinal Tap

Edina: Just for once, I want to take my clothes off and not be marked by them.

Absolutely Fabulous

Everyone in my class was enormous. They had to stop us doing cross-country running because we dented a viaduct.

Victoria Wood

I go in the dress shop and I ask this broad, "Have you got anything to make me look thinner?" She says, "Yeah, how's about a month in Bangladesh?"

Roseanne

I have flabby thighs, but fortunately my stomach covers them.

Joan Rivers

Kyle: Chef, we need Butters to gain about 50 pounds, fast.
Chef: Well, if you want him to get really fat as fast as possible, one of you will
      have to marry him.
Stan: Marry him?
Chef: It definitely worked for every woman I've ever met.

South Park

Sam: What are you up to, Norm?
Norm: My ideal weight... if I were 11 feet tall.

Cheers

The one thing I've learnt from watching Prisoner Cell Block H is that if they ever bring back hanging in Australia, they'd better get some bloody strong rope.

Frank Skinner

Edina: Inside of me, sweetie, inside of me, there is a thin person just screaming
      to get out.
Mother: Just the one, dear?

Absolutely Fabulous

There is an obesity epidemic. One out of every three Americans...
weighs as much as the other two.

Richard Jeni

When I was a child, I was so fat I was chosen to play Bethlehem in the school
nativity play.

Jo Brand

When you have a fat friend, there are no see-saws, only catapults.

Demetri Martin

FEAR

Rich Hall: I think fear smells like crab salad, 'cos I went into this deli the other
day and I said, "Could I have a crab salad sandwich, please?" and the woman
said, "We're all out of crab salad... I'm afraid."

QI

Some people are afraid of heights. Not me, I'm afraid of widths.

Steven Wright

FEMALE PROBLEMS

Elaine (talking about Louie's mother): What's wrong with her?
Louie: Female problems – she's starting not to look like one.

Taxi

FEMININITY

People say to me, "You're not very feminine." Well, they can just suck my dick.

Roseanne

FENG SHUI

Feng Shui: the ancient Chinese art of getting men to put the toilet lid down.

Jeff Green

FERTILITY

Scientists announced this week that a diet high in soy beans and high in soy sauce may reduce fertility in men. Which finally explains China's dreadfully low population.

Conan O'Brien

FIDGETING

Denise Royle: Dad, stop fiddling with yourself.
Jim Royle: I'm not fiddling with meself. I paid a quid for these underpants and I've got about 50 pence-worth stuck up me arse.

The Royle Family

FIRE

In elementary school, in case of fire you have to line up quietly in a single-file line from smallest to tallest. What's the logic? Do tall people burn slower?

Warren Hutcherson

Mrs Slocombe: Oh, I don't need a fire alarm. At the first sign of smoke, my pussy rushes into the garden and it sits on the concrete tortoise in the middle of the goldfish bowl.

Are You Being Served?

FISHING

Ralph: What are you fishing for?
Ted: Fish.

The Fast Show

Fish deserve to be caught, for they are lazy. Two million years of evolution and they still haven't got out of the water.

Simon Munnery

Give a man a fish; tomorrow, he's gonna want another fish. Teach a man to fish; tomorrow, he's standin' next to you on the dock catchin' your fish. Kill the man. Chop him to bits. Tomorrow, you got bait.

Basil White

FLAT EARTH

Will Hay: Well, Harbottle, you know the earth isn't flat, don't you?
Harbottle: It is where I live.

The Fourth Form At St Michael's

FLATULENCE

One time I was in this lift, crowded. Suddenly this bloke in the corner pipes up and he goes, "Oi! Who farted?" I said, "We all did at some point in our lives. Let's not start apportioning blame for individual farting, OK?" And he said, "It was you, was it?"

Simon Munnery

FLOWERS

I stooped to pick a buttercup. Why people leave buttocks lying around, I've no idea.

Stephen Fry

George: Grace, those are beautiful flowers. Where did they come from?
Gracie: Don't you remember, George? You said that if I went to visit Clara
    Bagley in the hospital I should be sure to take her flowers. So, when she
    wasn't looking, I did.

George Burns and Gracie Allen

Send a bunch of flowers to Mrs Upjohn and put "I love you" on the back of the bill.

Groucho Marx

FLYERS

Whenever I walk people try to hand me out flyers. And when someone tries to hand me out a flyer, it's kinda like they're saying: "Here, you throw this away."

Mitch Hedberg

FOOD

Hancock: That joint was harder when you took it out of the oven than when you put it in. That meal, whichever way you look at it, was a complete fiasco. I thought my mother was a bad cook, but at least her gravy used to move about.

Hancock's Half Hour (Sunday Afternoon At Home)

Does the expiration date on sour cream mean the date it becomes good?

Larry King

I bought a box of animal crackers and it said on it, "Do not eat if seal is broken." So I opened the box, and would you believe it…

Bob Monkhouse

I got myself a snack of low-sodium, low-fat Triscuits. If they were lower in anything else the box would be empty.

Tim Allen

I bought some powdered water, but I don't know what to add.

Steven Wright

I have a few business ideas and one of them is a service in which I offer to eat and describe pork to kosher people.

David Cross

In general, my children refuse to eat anything that hasn't danced on television.

Erma Bombeck

Master Heath (complaining to Basil about his dinner): These eggs look like you laid them.

Fawlty Towers

Miles: This stuff tastes awful. I could make a fortune selling it in my health food store.

Sleeper

Red meat is not bad for you. Now, blue-green meat, that's bad for you!

The Smothers Brothers

So I went down the local supermarket. I said "I want to make a complaint. This vinegar's got lumps in it." He said, "Those are pickled onions."

Tim Vine

The British love crap. We'll eat any crap going. Find a pig with dandruff and you've invented Pork Scratchings.

John Dowie

They say that food is the way to a man's heart. Bollocks! I think you'll find the way to a man's heart is through his hanky pocket with a breadknife. Why would you want to find your way to a man's heart anyway? It's not like there's a cake shop there.

Jo Brand

Hugh Dennis (asked to come up with 'things a TV chef would never say'): These Korean meatballs really are the dog's bollocks.

Mock the Week

This recipe is certainly silly. It says to separate two eggs, but it doesn't say how far to separate them.

Gracie Allen

Unlike European mustards that bring out the subtle flavours of food, English mustard makes your nose bleed.

Jack Dee

You ever dip your biscuit in your tea and it breaks? I swear, now, you never get used to that.

Peter Kay

FOREIGN LANGUAGES

English? Who needs that? I'm never going to England!

Homer Simpson

I bought a self-learning record to learn Spanish. I turned it on and went to sleep. During the night, the record skipped. The next day I could only stutter in Spanish.

Steven Wright

I speak Esperanto like a native.

Spike Milligan

Victor: What language are you talking in now? It appears to be Bollocks!

One Foot In the Grave

FOREIGNERS

World peace could be a possibility… if it weren't for all those damned foreigners!

Spike Milligan

You see, the thing about xenophobia is, it's a Greek word.

Al Murray (The Pub Landlord)

FOURTH OF JULY

What date does you hold the Fourth of July on?

Ali G

FRANCE

Boy, those French, they have a different word for everything!

Steve Martin

We shouldn't insult the French, of course, because they're not here to defend themselves. And we know how good they are at that!

Al Murray (The Pub Landlord)

FRIENDS

Bo: Am I amongst friends?
Eddy: Are you ever?

Absolutely Fabulous

Friends are like bras: close to your heart and there for support.

Richard Jeni

My friends tell me I have an intimacy problem. But they don't really know me.

Garry Shandling

FUN RUNS

"Fun" and "run" should never be in the same sentence. That's like saying, "Look at my humour tumour!"

Ardal O'Hanlon

FUNDAMENTALISM

All fundamentalists – Shiites, Moonies or Mormons – share the same belief: that you should live your life devoid of pleasure so you can go to Heaven when it's over. Which is basically like keeping your eyes shut through a movie in the hopes that you'll get your money back at the end.

A Whitney Brown

FUNERALS

Basil: Tie's a bit bright, isn't it, Major?
Major Gowen: What?
Basil: For a memorial service?
Major Gowen: Oh, I didn't like the chap.

Fawlty Towers

It was a catered funeral. It was held in a big hall with accordion players, and the buffet table was a replica of the deceased in potato salad.

Woody Allen

FURNITURE

I used to sell furniture for a living. The trouble was, it was my own.

Les Dawson

I was walking around a furniture shop last Saturday, and I was thinking, in this age of new inventions and technology it's disgraceful you still can't get a headboard with a toilet roll holder fitted.

Frank Skinner

GAMBLING

And the same six numbers came up the following week, so that was another three million... which was nice.

The Fast Show

I backed a horse today – 20 to one. It came in at 20 past four.

Tommy Cooper

I don't do the lottery, which means I'm marginally less likely to win than someone who does.

Linda Smith

I like to play blackjack. I'm not addicted to gambling. I'm addicted to sitting in a semi-circle.

Mitch Hedberg

I used to be a heavy gambler, but now I just make mental bets. That's how I lost my mind.

Steve Allen

My lucky number is four billion, which usually doesn't come in handy when you're gambling. "Come on, four billion…"

Mitch Hedberg

Playing poker online is like being mugged without the company.

Lucy Porter

GANGSTERS

So, I met this gangster who pulls up the back of people's pants. it was Wedgie Kray.

Tim Vine

GARDEN TOOLS

Pa Glum: Sorry to interrupt, but have you seen the garden shears? Mrs Glum wants to do her eyebrows.

Take It From Here

GAS

Anyway, to return to the joke which, as I was saying, was told to me by one of the gas company fellows – actually, the one they send round looking for gas leaks; the one with no eyebrows, the surprised expression and a box of matches…

Ronnie Corbett

GENIUS

A genius is a man who can rewrap a new shirt and not have any pins left over.

Dino Levi

Brent: If you were to ask me to name three geniuses, I probably wouldn't say Einstein, Newton... I'd go "Milligan, Cleese, Everett, Sessions."

The Office

He's a genius. He told me so himself.

Peter Cook

I remember when I posed as a customs officer so that I could meet Oscar Wilde. I said to him, "Have you anything to declare?" He said, "I have nothing to declare but my genius." I said, "I'll put that down as nothing, then, shall I?"

Simon Munnery

GEOGRAPHY

Magnus Magnusson: The next question is geographical. Is it possible for you to walk from Istanbul to Bangkok?
Sydney Bottocks: No.
Magnusson: Why not?
Bottocks: I've got a sore foot.
Magnusson: The answer is yes, you can make the entire journey without once passing water.
Bottocks: Not with my kidneys.

The Benny Hill Show

GEORGE BUSH

President Bush gave his first-ever presidential radio address in both English and Spanish. Reaction was mixed, however, as people were trying to figure out which one was which.

Dennis Miller

When the media ask George W Bush a question, he answers, "Can I use a lifeline?"

Robin Williams

GERMANS

Basil (taking a food order from his German guests): So, that's two egg mayonnaise, a prawn Goebbels, a Hermann Goering and four Colditz salads... Now, wait a minute. Well, I got a bit confused here. Sorry! I got a bit confused, 'cos everyone keeps mentioning the war. So, could you – what's the matter?

Elder Herr: Will you stop talking about the war?!

Basil: Me? You started it!

Elder Herr: We did not start it!

Basil: Yes, you did – you invaded Poland!

Fawlty Towers

I married a German. Every night I dress up as Poland and he invades me.

Bette Midler

Jeff Greene (with Suzie's German Shepherd dog): Boy, you seem to really like Oscar.

Larry: It's not every day that you get to be affectionate around something German; it just doesn't happen that often.

Curb Your Enthusiasm

My sister married a German. He complained he couldn't get a good bagel back home. I said: 'Well, whose fault is that?'

Emo Philips

GETTING UP EARLY

You've got to get up early in the morning to catch me peeking through your bedroom window.

Emo Philips

GHOST STORIES

Ronnie C: But now a sketch about ghosts and ghouls, in which I get caught by the ghosties.

Ronnie B: And I get caught by surprise.

The Two Ronnies

GIFTED CHILDREN

Alan: When did you first realise that Simon was abnormal?
John: Er, gifted, you mean?
Alan: Abnormally gifted.
John: Hmm. Well, it's when Simon was about 14 months old. I remember
looking at him there in his cot, and I said to him, "Who does Daddy love,
Simon? Who? Who?" And guess what Simon said?
Alan: What?
Simon: "Whom does Daddy love? Whom? Whom?"

Knowing Me, Knowing You

GLASGOW

The great thing about Glasgow is that if there's a nuclear attack it'll look exactly
the same afterwards.

Billy Connolly

GOD

If only God would give me some clear sign! Like making a large deposit in my
name at a Swiss bank.

Woody Allen

(From God's school report) Progress and conduct: I'm afraid that I am severley
disappointed in God's works. All three of Him have shown no tendency to
improve and He merely sits at the back of the class talking to himselves.
He has shown no interest in rugger, asked to be excused prayers and
moves in a mysterious way.

Monty Python's Brand New Bok

Eddy: I was taken up, sweetie. I spoke to God.
Saffy: What about?
Eddy: Well, shopping, mostly.

Absolutely Fabulous

Archie Bunker: God don't make mistakes. That's how He got to be God.

All In the Family

If God wanted us to believe in him... he'd exist!

Linda Smith

Not only is there no God, but try getting a plumber on weekends.

Woody Allen

GOD PARENTS

I'm a godmother. That's a great thing to be, a godmother. She calls me "God" for short. That's cute. I taught her that.

Ellen DeGeneres

GOING OUT

Brent: I don't know where we're going tonight. Obviously Finchy's a sophisticated guy, and Gareth's a culture vulture, so will it be opera, ballet, I don't know. I think the RSC's in town so, er... having said that, at Chasers it's 'Hooch for a pound and Wonder Bras get in free' night.

The Office

GOLDFISH

I used to have a goldfish. They're rubbish pets, aren't they? All they do is pace up and down and eat all day. In the end, I thought, "What he needs is a bit of exercise." I picked him up and threw him out on the lawn. He did about 30 sit-ups; that was it.

Jack Dee

GOLF

Golf is one of the few sports where a white man can dress like a black pimp and not look bad.

Robin Williams

I asked my good friend Arnold Palmer how I could improve my game. He advised me to cheat!

Bob Hope

Mainwaring: I've been trying to get in the golf club for years.
Wilson: Yes, well, they are rather particular, sir.

Dad's Army

Playing golf is like going to a strip joint. After 18 holes you're tired and most of
your balls are missing.

Tim Allen

GOOD AND BAD

Hitler was a bad man. Winston Churchill was a good man. But if you were in a
balloon with Hitler and Churchill, and you were losing altitude...

Harry Hill

THE GOOD LIFE

Vyvyan: NO, NO, NO, NO! WE ARE NOT WATCHING THE BLOODY GOOD
LIFE! BLOODY, BLOODY, BLOODY! I HATE IT! IT'S SO BLOODY NICE!
FELICITY "TREACLE TITS" KENDAL, AND RICHARD "SUGER-COATED SNOT"
BRIERS! WHAT DO THEY DO KNOW? CHOCOLATE BLOODY BUTTON
ADS, THAT'S WHAT! THEY'RE NOTHING BUT A COUPLE OF REACTIONARY
STEREOTYPES, CONFIRMING THE MYTH THAT EVERYONE IN BRITAIN IS A
LOVABLE MIDDLE-CLASS ECCENTRIC, AND I! HATE! THEM!

The Young Ones

GRAFFITI

Larry (after finding his house spray-painted by trick-or-treaters): They don't
deserve candy and I don't deserve this: "Bald Asshole"? That's a hate crime!

Curb Your Enthusiasm

Someone spray-painted a frowny face on my door. Then they tied a blank piece
of paper to a rock and threw it through the window. That'll teach me to make fun
of the illiterate.

Basil White

There's never any graffiti in the hotel, although in the gents' a couple of weeks a go I did see someone had drawn a lady's part. Quite detailed. The guy obviously had talent. That's the tragedy.

I'm Alan Partridge

GRATITUDE

For what you are about to receive, may the lord God make you truly grateful – as the bishop said to the actress.

Simon Munnery

I wish to thank my parents for making it all possible… and I wish to thank my children for making it necessary.

Victor Borge

Victor: Thank you, Saint Total Bastard, the patron saint of insurance companies.

One Foot In the Grave

GRAVITY

It's a good thing we have gravity, or else when birds died they'd just stay right up there.

Steven Wright

GUILT

My mother could make anybody feel guilty. She used to get letters of apology from people she didn't even know.

Joan Rivers

What is guilt? Guilt is the pledge drive constantly hammering in our heads that keeps us from fully enjoying the show. Guilt is the reason they put the articles in Playboy.

Dennis Miller

GYNAECOLOGY

A male gynaecologist is like an auto mechanic who's never owned a car.

Carrie Snow

My body's falling so fast my gynaecologist wears a hard hat.

Joan Rivers

HAIR

Anne Widdecombe's confused us all by going blonde. I was watching Question Time thinking, "Blimey, Sue Barker's slapped on a bit of weight."

Linda Smith

He doesn't dye his hair; he bleaches his face.

Johnny Carson

I just washed my hair. Now I cannae do a thing with the sink.

Billy Connolly

I know body hair bothers some women, but a lot of men like a fluffy partner.

Dame Edna Everage

I'm fascinated that hair grows after death. I'm looking forward to that.

Clive Anderson

The hair is real; it's the head that's fake.

Steve Allen

HAMMERS

If you nail a tool-shed closed, how do you put the hammer away?

George Carlin

HANGOVERS

Blackadder: Oh, God, God, God! What on earth was I drinking last night? My head feels like there's a Frenchman living in it.

Blackadder

I feel like I have a hangover, without all the happy memories and mystery bruises.

Ellen DeGeneres

What I never understand about a hangover is, where does the breath come from? You know what I mean? I mean, is someone shitting in your mouth?

Richard Pryor

HAPPINESS

Sybil: You're looking very happy, Basil.
Basil: Happy? Ah, yes, I remember that.

Fawlty Towers

Marjorie Dawes: You're obviously an incredibly unhappy person.
Barbara: No, I'm not!
Marjorie Dawes: Well, you deserve to be.

Little Britain

Naomi: I thought you were happy-go-lucky.
Jerry: No, no, no. I'm not happy, I'm not lucky and I don't go. If anything, I'm sad-stop-unlucky.

Seinfeld

I'm not renowned as someone with a happy-go-lucky, sparkling personality. I'm the man of whom Franz Kafka once remarked, "He's a miserable bastard, isn't he?"

John Dowie

What's the use of happiness? It can't buy you money.

Henny Youngman

Start every day off with a smile and get it over with.

W C Fields

I'm not worried. Apart from the pain and the agony I'm quite happy.

Hancock's Half Hour

HEALTH

Health nuts are going to feel stupid one day, lying in the hospital, dying of nothing.

Redd Foxx

A doctor has a stethoscope up to a man's chest. The man asks, "Doc, how do I stand?" The doctor says, "That's what puzzles me!"

Henny Youngman

According to this week's Time magazine, President George Bush is a serious fitness buff. He works out 60 to 90 minutes a day with weights. Apparently he likes working out because it 'clears his mind'. Sometimes it works a little too well.

Jay Leno

Doctor: You're AB negative.
Hancock: Is that bad?
Doctor: Oh, no, you're rhesus positive.
Hancock: Rhesus?! They're monkeys, aren't they? How dare you! What are you implying? I didn't come here to be insulted by a legalised vampire!

Tony Hancock (The Blood Donor)

Doctors are all crooks. There's no such thing as an honest doctor. Why do you think when a doctor operates he wears a mask? Why do you think they wear gloves? Sanitary reasons? Fingerprints!

Jackie Mason

Father: I must tell you that my boy is very delicate and there is something I would like to know: are your dormitories dry?
Headmaster: They are after 11pm; then they get drinks if they buy sandwiches.

Peter Sellers (Common Entrance)

First the doctor told me the good news: I was going to have a disease named after me.

Steve Martin

He's as strong as an ox, and almost as intelligent, sir. He has been personally inspected by Sister Anna from St John Thomas' Hospital, where she has a 90 per cent record of complete recovery – and that's in the mortuary.

The Benny Hill Show

I asked for some tests, but being the NHS they couldn't offer me an immediate appointment date, obviously, so what he offered to do was place my notes in a time capsule and conceal them under the surgery floorboards, which I thought was quite encouraging.

Helen Lederer

I know a man who gave up smoking, drinking, sex and rich food. He was healthy right up to the day he killed himself.

Johnny Carson

I told the doctor I broke my leg in two places. He told me to quit going to those places.

Henny Youngman

I walked into the surgery. The first thing the doctor did was remove the swelling from my wallet.

Morecambe and Wise

I went to the doctor's last week. I said, "Can I have some sleeping pills for the wife?" He said, "Why?" I said, "She's woken up."

Les Dawson

I went to the psychiatrist, and he says, "You're crazy." I tell him I want a second opinion. He says, 'Okay, you're ugly too!"

Rodney Dangerfield

If you ever have to go to the hospital, carry your own piss with you, 'cos that's what they want. Soon as you get to hospital, they want some blood and some piss. You always have the blood, but you never have the piss.

Richard Pryor

I'm ugly, I'm tellin' ya. My proctologist, he stuck his finger in my mouth.

Rodney Dangerfield

It's no longer a question of staying healthy. It's a question of finding a sickness you like.

Jackie Mason

My doctor's wonderful. Once, in 1955, when I couldn't afford an operation, he touched up the X-rays.

Joey Bishop

Never go to a doctor whose office plants have died.

Erma Bombeck

Nurse: "Doctor, the man you just gave a clean bill of health to dropped dead right as he was leaving the office."
Doctor: "Turn him around; make it look like he was walking in."

Henny Youngman

Rich Hall: Doctors use acronyms, such as GOMER – Get Out of My Emergency Room – or SARA – Sexual Activity-Related Accident.
Stephen Fry: There is one that doctors use in my part of the world, which is NFN – Normal For Norfolk.

QI

Sheila: I've got high blood pressure and water retention. You know what that gives you?
Bren: Boiling water?

Dinnerladies

Thanks to modern medicine we are no longer forced to endure prolonged pain, disease, discomfort and wealth.

Robert Orben

HEART PROBLEMS

Monica: You know, Phoebe, a heart attack is nature's way of telling you to slow down.
Chandler: I thought a heart attack was nature's way of telling you to die.

Friends

According to doctors, George Bush has the lowest heartbeat ever recorded by someone in the White House. Well, second lowest; Dick Cheney got his down to zero a couple of times.

Jay Leno

HECKLING

Stand-up comedy is the only art form to be heckled. Picasso never had two drunk guys in his studio yelling, "More green, idiot!"

Bill Maher

HELICOPTERS

A Polish man in a helicopter goes up to 800 feet. Down it comes! What happened? "It got chilly up there, so I turned off the fan!"

Henny Youngman

HELL

I was MARRIED for TWO FUCKING YEARS! Hell would be like Club Med!

Sam Kinison

HELP

Firefly: Rush to Freedonia. Three men and one woman are trapped in a building. Send help at once. If you can't send help, send two more women.

The Marx Brothers (Duck Soup)

HEROES

Brent: If there's one other person who's influenced me in that way, I think – someone who's a maverick, someone who does that to the system – then it's Ian Botham. Because Beefy will happily say, "That's what I think of your selection policy. Yes, I've hit the odd copper. Yes, I've enjoyed the odd doobie, but will you piss off and leave me alone? I'm walking to John O'Groats for some spastics."

The Office

HIP REPLACEMENT

After her accident, my nan had a plastic hip put in, but I thought they should have replaced it with a Slinky, 'cos if she did fall down the stairs again...

Steve Williams

HISTORY

I can't understand why I flunked American history. When I was a kid there was so little of it.

George Burns

My wife is a very ignorant woman. For years she thought the Charge of the Light Brigade was the electricity bill.

Les Dawson

HOLIDAYS

Alton Towers – the poor man's Disney, the sort of place you send a child who's dying of something not that serious.

Jimmy Carr

Honolulu – it's got everything: sand for the children, sun for the wife, sharks for the wife's mother.

Ken Dodd

HOME

I like to think of my house as nothing more than a glorified console for my television: the ultimate stereo cabinet.

Drew Carey

THE HOME SHOPPING NETWORK

I know a guy who called up the Home Shopping Network. They said, "Can I help you?" and he said, "No, I'm just looking."

George Miller

HOMELESSNESS

I'd like to help the homeless, but they're never home.

Lenny Clarke

I'm dating a homeless woman. It was easier talking her into staying over.

Garry Shandling

I'm going out with a homeless woman now. That's great. After a date you can drop her off anywhere.

Tom Dreesen

HOMO SAPIENS

Joey: If the Homo Sapiens were, in fact, Homo Sapiens... is that why they're extinct?
Ross: Homo Sapiens are people.
Joey: Hey, I'm not judging!

Friends

HOMOSEXUALITY

My first words: as I was being born, I looked up at my mother and said, "That's the last time I'm going up one of those."

Stephen Fry

You know you're gay if you bend over and see four balls.

Graham Norton

In my mind God made Adam and Eve; he didn't make Adam and Steve.

I'm Alan Partridge

Jim Royle: Elton John had a bloody wife, and he still dropped anchor in Pooh Bay.

The Royle Family

Homophobia is the irrational fear that three fags will break into your house and redecorate it against your will.

Tom Ammiano

Homosexuality in Russia is a crime and the punishment is seven years in prison, locked up with the other men. There is a three-year waiting list.

Yakov Smirnoff

Manny: I thought you were, actually. Gay, I mean.

Bernard: So did I, for a bit. Then I found out about the prohibitive standards of hygeine. And all that dancing!

Black Books

I once had a large gay following, but I ducked into an alley and lost him.

Emo Philips

HONEY

Bees make honey. It's so weird, because do earwigs make chutney? Do spiders make gravy?

Eddie Izzard

Like bees around honey. Why are bees so attracted to honey since they make it? It can only be vanity.

Simon Munnery

HORSE SENSE

Horse sense is the thing a horse has which keeps it from betting on people.

W C Fields

HOSTAGE TAKING

(During the time Terry Waite was being held hostage in Lebanon) Terry Waite – what a bastard! You lend some people a fiver, you never see them again.

Jerry Sadowitz

They say being a hostage is difficult, but I could do that with my hands tied behind my back.

Phil Nichol

HOTELS

I like staying in hotels. I enjoy hotels. I like tiny soap. I pretend that it's normal soap and my muscles are huge.

Jerry Seinfeld

A hotel mini-bar allows you to see into the future, and what a can of Pepsi will cost in 2020.

Rich Hall

Another of Robert Mugabe's former guerrilla commanders has been refused service in a Salisbury hotel for not wearing a tie. The manager was later sacked for not wearing a head.

Not the Nine O'Clock News

Mrs Richards (complaining about the view from her room window): When I pay for a view, I expect to see something more interesting than that.
Basil: That is Torquay, madam.
Mrs Richards: Well, that's not good enough.
Basil: Well, might I ask what you expected to see out of a Torquay hotel bedroom window? Sydney Opera House, perhaps? The hanging gardens of Babylon? Herds of wildebeest sweeping majestically...

Fawlty Towers

What's with this weird hotel custom of leaving a piece of chocolate on the pillow? I awoke thinking my brain had hemorrhaged some sort of fecal matter.

Jerry Seinfeld

This is an elegant hotel! Room service has an unlisted number.

Henny Youngman

Women like posh hotels; there's more for them to steal. Take them to a posh hotel and they all turn into the Artful Dodger.

Jeff Green

Room service? Send up a larger room!

Groucho Marx

HOUSEWORK

Harold: Look at it! When did you last clean this room out?
Albert: Yesterday.
Harold: Liar! Look at that.
Albert: It's only dust.

Harold: Dust? That's not dust; that's topsoil. If you leave it much longer we won't need a vacuum cleaner; we'll need a bleeding plough.

Steptoe and Son

Our house was that mucky, you had to wipe your feet before you went out.

Les Dawson

I hate housework. You make the beds, you wash the dishes and six months later you have to start all over again.

Joan Rivers

Carperpetuation: the act, when vacuuming, of running over a string at least a dozen times, reaching over and picking it up, examining it, then putting it back down to give the vacuum one last chance.

Rich Hall

HOW TO CONFUSE STRANGERS

Just go up to somebody on the street and say, "You're it!" and just run away.

Ellen DeGeneres

HOW TO DO IT

Alan: This week on "How to Do It" we're going to show you how to play the flute, how to split an atom, how to construct a box girder bridge, how to irrigate the Sahara Desert and make vast new areas of land cultivatable, but first, here's Jackie to tell you all how to rid the world of all known diseases.

Monty Python's Flying Circus

HUNTING

Hunting is not a sport. In a sport, both sides should know they're in the game.

Paul Rodriguez

I ask people why they have deer heads on their walls. They always say, because it's such a beautiful animal. I think my mother is attractive, but I have photographs of her.

Ellen DeGeneres

HYPNOTISM

Kenny Craig: Look into my eyes, look into my eyes, the eyes, the eyes, not around the eyes, don't look around the eyes, look into my eyes, you're under. I have not been taking your underwear home, putting it on in my bedroom and then parading up and down in front of the mirror going, "Oh, oh, oh, oh". Three, two, one... You're back in the room.

Little Britain

I CAN'T BELIEVE IT'S NOT BUTTER

Alice (getting confused over various butter-like spreads): Well, I can't believe I Can't Believe It's Not Butter and the stuff I can't believe is not I Can't Believe It's Not Butter is not butter. I believe that they both just might in fact be butter, but in cunning disguises, and in fact there's a lot more butter out there than we believe.

The Vicar of Dibley

ICE CREAM

Samantha has to go now as she's off to meet her Italian gentleman friend who's taking her out for an ice-cream. She says she likes nothing better than to spend the evening licking the nuts off a large Neopolitan.

I'm Sorry I Haven't A Clue

IDENTIFICATION

Monica: You must be Louie.
Louie: How did you know my name?
Monica: I only had three people described to me. One was smart, one was good-looking and one was you.

Taxi

You might recognise me. I'm the fourth guy from the left on the evolutionary chart.

Jay London

ILLEGAL IMMIGRANTS

America – 20 Million Illegal Immigrants Can't Be Wrong!

Richard Jeni

If you want to live in America, don't sneak over the borders. Do it the right way; get adopted by Angelina Jolie.

Jimmy Kimmel

Illegal aliens have always been a problem in the United States. Ask any Indian.

Robert Orben

IDENTITY

Peerless Pauline: I've waited so long to find someone like you.
J Cheever Loophole: Oh, someone like me? I'm not good enough for you, eh?

The Marx Brothers (At the Circus)

I was on the street. This guy waved to me, and he came up to me and said, "I'm sorry, I thought you were someone else." And I said, "I am."

Demetri Martin

I don't need to worry about identity theft because no one wants to be me.

Jay London

If you'd been where I've been, if you've seen the things I've seen… you'd be me… or someone following me around.

Simon Munnery

IMITATION

Imitation is the sincerest form of television.

Fred Allen

IMMORTALITY

I don't want to achieve immortality through my work. I want to achieve immortality by not dying.

Woody Allen

IMPEACHMENT

Bush is smart. I don't think that Bush will ever be impeached, 'cos unlike Clinton, Reagan or even his father, George W is immune from scandal. Because, if George W testifies that he had no idea what was going on, wouldn't you believe him?

Jay Leno

INADEQUACIES

Eleanor: You remember the other night you asked me what Geoffrey could give me that you can't?
John: Yes.
Eleanor: Well, I've made a list.

Eleanor Bron and John Fortune

INDIVIDUALITY

Steve Martin: Now let's repeat the non-conformists' oath: I promise to be different!
Audience: I promise to be different!
Steve: I promise to be unique!
Audience: I promise to be unique!
Steve: I promise not to repeat things other people say!.. Good!

Steve Martin

INFAMY

Julius Caesar: Infamy, infamy! They've all got it in for me!
Carry On Cleo (although originally from 1950s radio series Take It From Here)

INNOCENCE

Pete: Adam and Eve, while they were in the Garden of Eden, they didn't have anything to do with sex to start with, you know. When they were in Paradise they didn't have anything to do with sex 'cos they were wandering around naked but they didn't know they were naked.

Dud: I bet they did know. I mean, you'd soon know once you got caught on the brambles.

Peter Cook and Dudley Moore.

INSANITY

My brother thinks he's a chicken; we don't talk him out of it because we need the eggs.

Groucho Marx

Patient: I am a rabbit.

Psychiatrist: If you were a rabbit you'd have great big long ears!

Patient: They must have dropped off!

Psychiatrist: Don't be so stupid! If you say you're a rabbit once more, I'll smash your teeth in! Now what are you?

Patient: I'm... er ... er... a dog!

Psychiatrist: That's better! We'll take it from there next week.

At Last The 1948 Show

Blackadder: He's mad. He's mad! He's madder than Mad Jack McMad, the winner of this year's Mr Madman competition.

Blackadder

They say the definition of insanity is doing the same thing over and over and expecting a different result. And unfortunately, it is also the definition of Canadian politics.

Rick Mercer

You know the world is going crazy when the best rapper is a white guy, the best golfer is a black guy, the tallest guy in the NBA is Chinese, the Swiss hold the America's Cup, France is accusing the US of arrogance, Germany doesn't want to go to war and the three most powerful men in America are named 'Bush', 'Dick', and 'Colon'.

Chris Rock

INSECTS

Patsy: The last mosquito that bit me had to book into the Betty Ford Clinic.

Absolutely Fabulous

It's only when you look at an ant through a magnifying glass on a sunny day that you realise how often they burst into flames.

Harry Hill

In the South Pacific, because of their size, mosquitoes are required to file flight plans.

Erma Bombeck

Ant expert (waving arms around to explain how an ant communicates): It's signalling! It's signalling! He's saying: "Give us a hand with this small vole!"...
Interviewer: How do you know he's saying: "Give us a hand with this small vole"? I mean, it's so specific.
Ant expert: Well, I'm not a bloody ant, am I? How should I know what a bloody ant says? WHO CARES WHAT A BLOODY ANT SAYS?

At Last The 1948 Show

Did you know that if a stick insect laid its eggs in a jar of Bovril, it will give birth to a litter of Twiglets?

Tim Vine

I sort of felt sorry for the damn flies. They never hurt anybody. Even though they were supposed to carry disease, I never heard anybody say he caught anything from a fly. My cousin gave two guys the clap, and nobody ever whacked her with a newspaper.

Lenny Bruce

INSTRUCTION MANUALS

I have a car stereo that will leave messages. It's got a manual two inches thick. The manual that came with my wife is smaller.

Tim Allen

INSULTS

Christine: You're quite shallow, aren't you? No offence meant!
Bren: No, but lots taken.

Dinnerladies

Blackadder: Baldrick, go forth into the streets and announce that Lord Blackadder wishes to sell his house. Percy, just go forth into the streets.

Blackadder

Bernard (to Manny): You know what you are? You're a beard with an idiot hanging off it.

Black Books

Blackadder: You're about as useful as a one-legged man at an arse-kicking contest.

Blackadder

Carla: If you can't say anything nice – say it about Diane.

Cheers

Do you think I can buy back my introduction to you?

Groucho Marx

Dreyfus: Compared to Clouseau, Attila the Hun was a Red Cross volunteer!

Return of the Pink Panther

Flo: Why, I've never been so insulted in my life!
Dr Hugo Hackenbush: Well, it's early yet.

The Marx Brothers (A Day At the Races)

I didn't come here to be insulted. I could have stayed at home and read my fan mail.

Morecambe and Wise

I don't wanna talk to you no more, you empty-headed animal food trough-wiper! I fart in your general direction! Your mother was a hamster and your father smelt of elderberries!

Monty Python and the Holy Grail

I've had a perfectly wonderful evening – but this wasn't it.

Groucho Marx

I never forget a face, but in your case I'll make an exception.

Groucho Marx

I thought that I saw your name on a bag of bread, but when I reread it, it said: "Thick Cut".

Jack Dee

Jim Hacker: Humphrey, do you see it as part of your job to help ministers make fools of themselves?
Sir Humphrey: Well, I never met one that needed any help.

Yes, Minister

Lilith: I described you in terms which were positively glowing, which is exactly how I'd like to see you in Hell.

Cheers

Louie: Do you know what the difference is between people like you and people like me, Nardo?
Alex: Yeah: two million years of evolution.

Taxi

Mary: You've a face like a pair o' tits!
John: At least that's one pair between us!

Father Ted

Nana: May God forgive you, Jim Royle, for talking ill of the dead like that.
Jim: I wasn't speaking ill of the dead. I was speaking about you: the living bloody dead!

The Royle Family

Ralph: You're the type of person that would bend waaaaay over to pick up a penny on the sidewalk. I wouldn't.
Alice: You couldn't.

The Honeymooners

Robin Day: I didn't come here to be insulted.
Eric: Where do you normally go?

Morecambe and Wise

You know, I could rent you out as a decoy for duck-hunters?

Groucho Marx

You look like something the dog just buried in the backyard and is trying to forget where.

Milton Berle

She said: "Would you like to see me in something flowing?" I said, "Yes –
the River Thames."

Morecambe and Wise

Stantz (indicating Peck): Everything was fine until our power grid was shut off by
    dickless here.
Walter Peck (protesting): They caused the explosion!
Mayor: Is this true?
Venkman: Yes, it's true… this man has no dick.

Ghostbusters

INSURANCE

I've got gorgeous legs. They're insured for skillions. I don't know what part of
Madonna is insured: perhaps the gap between her teeth.

Edna Everage

The insurance man callled this morning and said if the last instalment on your
granny's funeral isn't paid, up she comes!

Frank Carson

INTELLIGENCE AND THE LACK OF IT

Ernie: What's the matter with you?
Eric: I'm an idiot. What's your excuse?

Morecambe and Wise

127

Wanda: To call you stupid would be an insult to stupid people. I've known sheep that could outwit you. I've worn dresses with higher IQs!

A Fish Called Wanda

Blackadder: George, who is using the family brain cell at the moment?

Blackadder

Holly: I am Holly, the ship's computer, with an IQ of 6,000, the same IQ as 6,000 PE teachers.

Red Dwarf

Alan Davies: I'm not as stupid as you think!
Stephen Fry: No, you're not. You couldn't be.

QI

I wish I was like you! You know: startled by direct sunlight.

Dylan Moran

Is being an idiot like being high all the time?

Janeane Garofalo

Arthur: You'll have to forgive Hank. His heart's in the right place but he keeps his brain in a box at home.

The Larry Sanders Show

David St Hubbins: It's such a fine line between stupid and clever.

Spinal Tap

Firefly: Gentlemen, Chicolini here may talk like an idiot, and look like an idiot, but don't let that fool you. He really is an idiot.

The Marx Brothers (Duck Soup)

Holly: An IQ of six? Do me a lemon! That's a poor IQ for a glass of water!

Red Dwarf

If stupidity got us into this mess, then why can't it get us out?

Will Rogers

If you read a lot of books you are considered well read, but if you watch a lot of TV you're not considered well viewed.

Lily Tomlin

Some people are so dumb, they think the number before 0 is blast-off.

Dennis Regan

The Clinton White House today said they would start to give national security and intelligence briefings to George Bush. I don't know how well this is working out. Today, after the first one, Bush said: "I've got one question; what colour is the red phone?"

Bill Maher

The White House is giving George W Bush intelligence briefings... you know, some of these jokes just write themselves.

David Letterman

Think of how stupid the average person is, and realise half of them are stupider than that.

George Carlin

INTERNATIONAL POLITICS

Jim Hacker: Apparently, the White House thinks that the Foreign Office is full of pinkoes and traitors.
Bernard: No, it's not: well, not full.

Yes, Minister

Jim Hacker: Who knows Foreign Office secrets, apart from the Foreign Office?
Bernard: That's easy: only the Kremlin.

Yes, Minister

Prime Minister Harold Macmillan: I went first to Germany and there I spoke with the German Foreign Minister, Herr... Herr and there. And we exchanged many frank words in our respective languages.

Peter Cook (Beyond the Fringe)

Ronald Reagan (having just passionately kissed Margaret Thatcher): Nice gal. Shame I'm only screwing her country!

Spitting Image

INTERVIEW TECHNIQUE

Alan: Now, you are a celebrity; you're France's second-best racing driver; you get interviewed all the time. Do you get bored of the same old questions?

Michel: Yes, that's very true; there's nothing worse than an interviewer who cannot be bothered to find an interesting angle.

Alan: Yeah, I can imagine. When did you first want to be a racing driver?

Knowing Me, Knowing You

INTRUDERS

Dutch Gunderson: Who are you and how did you get in here?
Frank Drebin: I'm a locksmith – and I'm a locksmith.

Police Squad

INVASION

The missus looked at me and she said, "What are you supposed to be?" I said, "Supposed to? I'm one of the Home Guards." She said, "One of the Home…?" She said, "What're the others like?" And then the missus said, "Well, what d'yer do in the Home Guards?" I said, "I've got to stop Hitler's army landing." She said, "What – you?" I said, "No... there's Harry Bates and Charlie Evans and.... there's seven or eight of us altogether."

Robb Wilton

IRAQ

Well, we won the war. You know what that means; in 20 years, we'll all be driving Iraqi cars.

Will Durst

CNN said that after the war there is a plan to divide Iraq into three parts: regular, premium and unleaded.

Jay Leno

You know we armed Iraq? I wondered about that too. You know during the Persian Gulf war, those intelligence reports would come out: "Iraq: incredible weapons – incredible weapons." How do you know that? "Uh, well... we looked at the receipts."

Bill Hicks

President Bush said that he is worried that Iraq could be overrun by religious fundamentalists. Hey, if it's good enough for the Republican Party, it's good enough for Iraq.

Jay Leno

IRELAND

Irish people love Muslims. They've taken a lot of heat off us. Before, we were "the terrorists" but now, we're "the Riverdance people".

Andrew Maxwell

IRONY

Remember that song 'Ironic'? No, it's not. She kept naming all these things in the song that were meant to be ironic and none of them were. They were all just unfortunate. The song should have been called 'Unfortunate'. The only ironic thing about that song is that it's called 'Ironic' and it's written by a woman who doesn't know what 'ironic' means. Now that's quite ironic.

Ed Byrne

JAPANESE

Seems ages since I had a natter with old Yoko Suji in Tokyo. I wonder how his wife is, what was her name? "Radiant Flower Of The Divine Heavens". I wonder if her feet are still playing her up.

Hancock (The Radio Ham)

JEALOUSY OF OTHER WOMEN

Mel: I tell you, she was even jealous of me and Nellie.
Griff: Not Smelly Nellie, the fat bird down the Goat and Anchor?
Mel: Yeah.
Griff: Corfhhh!
Mel: Her mum, she was jealous of her.
Griff: Never!
Mel: And your Aunt Madge.
Griff: No!
Mel: I kid you not... and those were just ones I did have it off with.

Smith and Jones

JEREMY

Stephen Fry: Have you met an American Jeremy?
Jeremy Clarkson: No. It's too complicated: three syllables.

QI

JEWELLERY

Many of my friends are getting engaged and are buying diamonds for their fiancée. What better to symbolise marriage than the hardest thing known to man?

Mike Dugan

JEWISH

I'm a Jew, by the way. It was my agent's idea.

Simon Amstell

Archie Bunker: Jesus was a Jew, yes, but only on his mother's side.

All In the Family

I had left home (like all Jewish girls) in order to eat pork and take birth control pills. When I first shared an intimate evening with my husband I was swept away by the passion (so dormant inside myself) of a long and tortured existence, the physical cravings I had tried so hard to deny finally and ultimately sated... but enough about the pork.

Roseanne

I was raised half Jewish and half Catholic. When I'd go to confession, I'd say "Bless me, father, for I have sinned – and you know my attorney, Mr Cohen?"

Bill Maher

If you live in New York, even if you're Catholic, you're Jewish.

Lenny Bruce

JIGGERY-POKERY

Frederick Carver: Oh, come, come, Stoppidge; you know as well as I that all young doctors indulge in a bit of jiggery-pokery.
Dr Stoppidge: Sir, I do not object to jiggery, but I take exception to pokery!

Carry On Again Doctor

JIGSAWS

I wanna make a jigsaw puzzle that's 40,000 pieces, and when you finish it, it says, "Go outside."

Demetri Martin

JOAN OF ARC

They laughed at Joan of Arc, but she went right ahead and built it.

Gracie Allen

JOHN LENNON

We live in a country where John Lennon takes six bullets in the chest. Yoko Ono was standing right next to him – not ONE FUCKING BULLET! Explain that to me, God!

Denis Leary

JOKES AND COMEDY

What is comedy? Comedy is the art of making people laugh without making them puke.

Steve Martin

Definition of a comedian: a guy with a good memory who hopes no one else has.

Red Skelton

Three blind mice walk into a pub… but they are all unaware of their surroundings, so to derive humour from it would be exploitative.

Bill Bailey

Everything is funny as long as it is happening to somebody else.

Will Rogers

Tragedy is when I cut my finger. Comedy is when you walk into an open sewer and die.

Mel Brooks

There's so much comedy on television. Does that cause comedy in the streets?

Dick Cavett

Some jokes are short and elegant, like a mathematical proof or a midget in a ballgown.

Demetri Martin

JOURNALISM

I only believe the date in the papers these days.

Lily Savage

After a marriage lasting only seven days a newspaper editor's wife has filed a petition for divorce on the grounds that he is too small a type, she's become bored with his special features and he refuses to give her a late-night extra.

The Two Ronnies

JUNGLE EXPLORATION

Captain Cleese: Three days later, the jungle was behind us – in front of us and all around us. Then our food ran out.

[Footsteps]

Bill Oddie: Come back, food!

I'm Sorry, I'll Read That Again

KIDNAPPING

I remember the time I was kidnapped and they sent a piece of my finger to my father. He said he wanted more proof.

Rodney Dangerfield

When I was a kid I got no respect. The time I was kidnapped, and the kidnappers sent my parents a note, they said: "We want five thousand dollars or you'll see your kid again."

Rodney Dangerfield

KILTS

Is there anything worn under the kilt? No, it's all in perfect working order.

Spike Milligan

KINDERGARTEN

I was coming home from kindergarten… well, they told me it was kindergarten. I found out later I'd been working in a factory for ten years. It's good for a kid to know how to make gloves.

Ellen DeGeneres

KISSING

Andre Melly: You kissed her when she least expected it.
Mervyn Cruddy: I beg your pardon?
Andre: You kissed her when she least expected it.
Mervyn Cruddy: Oh, I thought you said "where".

The Benny Hill Show

Eric (as Cyrano de Bergerac): What would it take for you to kiss me?
Penelope Keith (as the Queen of France): Chloroform.

Morecambe and Wise

I wasn't kissing her, I was just whispering in her mouth.

Chico Marx

LACTOSE INTOLERANCE

My whole family is lactose-intolerant and when we take pictures we can't say "Cheese".

Jay London

LANGUAGE

I had a linguistics professor who said that it's man's ability to use language that makes him the dominant species on the planet. That may be, but I think there's one other thing that separates us from animals; we aren't afraid of vacuum cleaners.

Jeff Stilson

I personally think we developed language because of our deep need to complain.

Lily Tomlin

LAW

A man calls a lawyer's office. The phone is answered: "Schwartz, Schwartz, Schwartz and Schwartz." The man says, "Let me talk to Mr Schwartz." "I'm sorry: he's on vacation." "Then let me talk to Mr Schwartz." "He's on a big case: not available for a week." "Then let me talk to Mr Schwartz." "He's playing golf today." "OK, then let me talk to Mr Schwartz." "Speaking."

Henny Youngman

My attorney is brilliant. He didn't bother to graduate from law school. He settled out of class.

Milton Berle

The word "testify" actually comes from the ancient Roman practice of men – when they were in court swearing an oath, they had to clutch their testicles – it's true! And it does work, I've found. If you clutch a bloke's testicles quite hard, he swears an oath.

Jo Brand

Jon Culshaw (asked to come up with 'something ill-advised to say in court'): If I'm found not guilty, can I keep all the stuff I nicked?

Mock the Week

Getting out of jury duty is easy. The trick is to say you're prejudiced against all races.

Homer Simpson

Juries scare me. I don't want to put my faith in 12 people who weren't smart enough to get out of jury duty.

Monica Piper

Being a miner, as soon as you're too old and tired and ill and sick and stupid to do the job properly, you have to go. Well, the very opposite applies with judges.

Peter Cook

LAZINESS

Richie: Come on, it's Sunday; it's a day of rest! Absolutely nothing to do for 24 hours.
Eddie: It's a bit like every other day then, really, isn't it?

Bottom

As it is, I have to negotiate with myself just to get out of bed. "All right, here's the deal, me: I'll get up, but I'm not taking a fucking shower. That's something we'll negotiate later on."

Jim Gaffigan

A young boy shouldn't be given up for hopeless just because he's lazy, surly and good for nothing. Don't be discouraged by those things; maybe he's just trying to be like his daddy.

Gracie Allen

The laziest man I ever met put popcorn in his pancakes so they'd turn over by themselves.

W C Fields

> You ever got one thing to do all day but you just can't get yourself to do it? "I gotta go to the post office... but I'd probably have to put on pants. They're only open until five. I'm going to have to do that next week."
>
> *Jim Gaffigan*

LEARNING TO DRIVE

How far had Mr Adams gotten in the lesson?... "Backing out." I see. You were backing out at 75 and that's... that's when he jumped... Did he cover starting the car? And the other way of stopping? What's the other way of stopping? "Throwing it in reverse."

Bob Newhart (The Driving Instructor)

Three weeks ago, she learned how to drive. Last week she learned how to aim it.

Henny Youngman

Now, what's the first thing we're going to do before we pull out into traffic? What did Mr Adams do before he let you pull out into traffic? Well, I mean besides praying...

Bob Newhart (The Driving Instructor)

LEARNING TO WRITE

You go to learn to write in first grade. They give you this grade triple Z paper with big hunks of wood still floating around in it. You got to write around the big hunks of wood. The lines are about eight feet apart. They don't want you to miss getting in between the lines. They give these pencils as big as a horse's leg and you rest them on your shoulder as you write. "A... B... May I have another piece of paper, please?"

Bill Cosby

LEAVING

Firefly: You can leave in a taxi. If you can't leave in a taxi, you can leave in a huff. If that's too soon, you can leave in a minute and a huff.

The Marx Brothers (Duck Soup)

Mrs Spooner: I'm leaving you.

The Reverend Spooner: What do you mean?

Mrs Spooner: It's quite simple, William. I can't spoon any more Standerisms!

The Two Ronnies

Go, and never darken my towels again!

Groucho Marx

LESBIANS

George: I have a bad feeling that whenever a lesbian looks at me they think: "That's why I'm not a heterosexual."

Seinfeld

Some men think that they can convert gay women, and turn them straight. No way could I do that – but I could make straight women gay.

Jeff Tilson

I'm sick of fellas. Think I'll become a lesbian. At least you get to wear flat shoes.

Lily Savage

Jeff: Oh, wouldn't that be great... being a lesbian? All the advantages of being a man, but with less embarrassing genitals.

Coupling

LETTERS

First-class stamps are to go up to 15p from next week. That's 2p for postage and 13p for storage.

Not the Nine O'Clock News

Ever get a letter and you aren't sure who it's from? Run after the postman and shout, "1471". He'll have to tell you.

Harry Hill

LIFE

Trillian: That's just fine, really... just part of life.
Marvin: Life. Don't talk to me about life.

The Hitchhiker's Guide To the Galaxy

Coach: How's life treating you, Norm?
Norm: Like it caught me in bed with its wife.

Cheers

I wanna live 'til I die, no more, no less.

Eddie Izzard

I was high on life, but eventually I built up a tolerance.

Arj Barker

Bush reiterated his stand to conservatives opposing his decision on stem cell research. He said today he believes life begins at conception and ends at execution.

Jay Leno

LIKES AND DISLIKES

If there's one thing I can't bear, it's when hundreds of old men come creeping in through the window in the middle of the night and throw all manner of garbage all over me. I can't bear that.

Peter Cook

LINCONSHIRE POACHER

Rambling Syd Rumpo (to the tune of "The Lincolnshire Poacher"):
When I was a clencher's bogle man in famous Lincoln Town,
I often clenched my bogling fork for less than half a crown.
And I would woggle and nurk, my boys, as I shall quickly tell,
Oh... 'tis my delight on a shining night and a foggy night as well!

Round the Horne

LIONEL BLAIR

People say, "Ooh, doesn't Lionel Blair look good for his age?" Well, no, not really. Not unless he's about five hundred. Otherwise he looks like nothing more than an elaborately coiffured scrotum.

Linda Smith

LOANS

My neighbour asked if he could use my lawnmower and I told him of course he could, so long as he didn't take it out of my garden.

Morecambe and Wise

THE LOCH NESS MONSTER

According to a recent survey the Loch Ness Monster is the world's most unexplained mystery. Or, as the Scots call it, "The weather's-shit-we-need-something-to-bring-in-the-tourists-Ness monster."

Jimmy Carr

LOLLIPOP LADIES

My mum was a lollipop lady – by which I mean she had a very thin body and a big, round, red, sticky head.

Harry Hill

LONDON UNDERGROUND

The first Tube station built was Baker Street in 1863. What was the point of that? Where would you go?

Paul Merton

LONELY HEARTS

I once placed an advert in a Lonely Hearts column: "Second Person Required For Suicide Pact."

John Dowie

Eddie: Why not put an ad in the Lonely Hearts column?
Richie: Yeah!
Eddie: Yeah, yeah: "Ugly virgin desperately seeks sex of any description."

Bottom

LOOKING ON THE BRIGHT SIDE

Victor: I'll try counting my blessings... well, that didn't take very long.

One Foot In the Grave

Brent: We all wake up and we go, "Oh, I ache; I'm not 18 any more, you know, I'm thirty ni – you know, I'm in my thirties, I'm not...", but so what? At least I've got my health. And if you haven't got your health... if you've got one leg, at least I haven't got two legs missing. And if you have lost both legs and both arms, just go, "At least I'm not dead!"

The Office

Victor: I wonder what bounteous joys the rest of the week has in store. Bubonic plague? Nest of scorpions in the Hoover bag?

One Foot In the Grave

LOOKING ON THE DOWN SIDE

Things are going to get a lot worse before they get worse.

Lily Tomlin

Bloodnok: What's the matter with you this morning, Seagoon? Why have you got such a long face?
Seagoon: Heavy dentures, sir.

The Goon Show

I always get screwed by the system. That's my place in the universe. I'm the system's bitch.

Drew Carey

I'm so unlucky that if I was to fall into a barrel of nipples I'd come out sucking my thumb.

Freddie Starr

Piano accompaniment will be provided by Colin Sell. Actually, we've realised after all these years that, when it comes to choosing a pianist, Colin is one in a million... yes, really, how unlucky can you get?

I'm Sorry I Haven't A Clue

I guess I just prefer to see the dark side of things. The glass is always half-empty. And cracked. And I just cut my lip on it. And chipped a tooth.

Janeane Garofalo

Harold: I know what we'll do. We'll collect up all the scrap we can find...
Albert: Yeah.
Harold: Lead piping, brass, copper, iron . . .
Albert: Yeah.
Harold: Fill all our pockets up with it... and jump in the canal.
Albert: Don't talk silly, Harold.
Harold: Why not? It's better than living like this. It wouldn't take long. I'll lay on top of you.

Steptoe and Son

LOQUACIOUSNESS

Firefly: You haven't stopped talking since I came here! You must have been vaccinated with a phonograph needle!

The Marx Brothers (Duck Soup)

Frasier: You're a psychiatrist. You know what it's like to listen to people prattling on endlessly about their mundane lives.
Niles: Touché. And on that subject, I heard your show today.

Frasier

Diane: Sam, may I have a brief word with you?
Sam: I suppose you could, but I doubt it.

Cheers

Frasier: The man talks endlessly on subjects that are of no interest to anyone but him.
Niles: Gee. I can't imagine what that's like.

Frasier

LOST AND FOUND

I believe in honesty. I once found a wallet with £300 in it. Did I keep it? I did not. I went right out and put an ad in the Lost and Found column of the Budapest Daily News.

Morecambe and Wise

I was walking down Fifth Avenue today and I found a wallet. I was gonna keep it, rather than return it, but I thought: well, if I lost $150, how would I feel? And I realised I would want to be taught a lesson.

Emo Philips

I was walking down the street and saw a sign on a post. It said, "Reward. Lost: $50. If found, just keep it."

Steven Wright

LOVE

I recently sold the rights of my love life to Parker Brothers and they're going to turn it into a game.

Woody Allen

A lot of people wonder how you can tell if you're really in love. Just ask yourself this question: "Would I mind being financially destroyed by this person?"

Ronnie Shakes

Dr Hugo Hackenbush: She's so in love with me, she doesn't know anything. That's why she's in love with me.

The Marx Brothers (A Day At the Races)

Frank: I've finally found someone I can love – a good, clean love... without utensils.

The Naked Gun

I know that there are people who do not love their fellow-man, and I hate people like that!

Tom Lehrer

If love is the answer, could you please rephrase the question?

Lily Tomlin

Money is not the most important thing in the world. Love is. Fortunately, I love money.

Jackie Mason

The difference between love and lust is that lust never costs over $200.

Johnny Carson

This year, I will hug my wife more – or have my assistant hug her more for me.

Ray Romano

LOW SELF-ESTEEM

Donald: You know what you are? You're a self-loathing Jew.
Larry: Hey, I may loathe myself, but it has nothing to do with the fact that I'm Jewish.

Curb Your Enthusiasm

I told my psychiatrist that everyone hates me. He said I was being ridiculous; everyone hasn't met me yet.

Rodney Dangerfield

Sometimes I get the feeling that the whole world is against me, but deep down I know that's not true. Some of the smaller countries are neutral.

Robert Orben

LOYALTY

I'm very loyal in relationships. Even when I go out with my mom I don't look at other moms.

Garry Shandling

LYING

Chicolini: Well, who you gonna believe: me or your own eyes?

The Marx Brothers (Duck Soup)

MAKE-UP

I consider myself very fortunate. I owe everything to my family and my make-up man. My wonderful family keeps me going and my wonderful make-up man keeps me from looking like I already went.

Bob Hope

I have this terrific make-up man, but he's expensive. I have to bring him in from Lourdes.

Bob Hope

Lisa: I couldn't get her to take off her make-up...
Drew: I heard they tried once, and there was a whole other painting underneath it.

The Drew Carey Show

What an amazing place: the Clinique counter. The women are wearing white laboratory jackets. I'm thinking there's some serious stuff going on here! What have they got: girls in the back on stretchers, OD'd on mascara?

Kit Hollerbach

MAKING A SPEECH

Speaking in front of a crowd is considered the number one fear of the average person. I found that amazing. Number two was death! That means, to the average person, if you have to be at a funeral, you would rather be in the casket than doing the eulogy.

Jerry Seinfeld

MARINE LIFE

Have you heard about the oyster who went to a disco and pulled a mussel?

Billy Connolly

The North Atlantic sperm whale grows up to 100 feet – which it uses to walk across the seabed like a giant centipede.

Alexei Sayle

I'm afraid of sharks, but only in a water situation.

Demetri Martin

The next round is Sound Charades, based on the erstwhile TV favourite Give Us A Clue, the true master of which was Lionel Blair. No one who witnessed the event will ever forget the sparkle in Lionel Blair's eye as he received Free Willy from Michael Aspel for two minutes!

I'm Sorry I Haven't A Clue

MARRIAGE

Basil: Did you ever see that film How To Murder Your Wife?
Major Gowen: How To Murder Your Wife?
Basil: Yes. Awfully good. I saw it six times...

Fawlty Towers

Marriage is a great institution, but I'm not ready for an institution yet.

Mae West

Marriage is a wonderful invention; then again, so is a bicycle repair kit.

Billy Connolly

If variety is the spice of life, marriage is the big can of leftover Spam.

Johnny Carson

Before you get married, I want you to make me a promise. I want you to remember this face: AAAAAAAAAAAAAAAAAAAAAAA AAARRUUGH!!!!!!!!!

Sam Kinison

I'm in the business of making people laugh and making people happy. I don't set out to do it. It's people. They just can't help laughing when they see me and I'm not embarrassed by that. I think it's rather sexy. As a matter of fact, my husband used to laugh. In fact, on my honeymoon he never stopped laughing.

Dame Edna Everage

Basil: Sybil, do you remember when we were first manacled together, we used to laugh quite a lot?
Sybil: Yes, Basil, but not at the same time.

Fawlty Towers

I honestly thought my marriage would work because me and my wife did share a sense of humour. We had to, really, because she didn't have one.

Frank Skinner

My marriage was my dad's idea. She was the girl next door and her father had an electric drill.

Ronnie Corbett

Matron: No, I have no urge to marry you.
Gladstone Screwer: Oh, no, don't worry about that – the urge comes later!

Carry On Again Doctor

Sir Arthur: I met my wife during the war. She blew in through the drawing-room window with a bit of shrapnel, became embedded in the sofa and one thing led to her mother and we were married within the hour.

Peter Cook and Dudley Moore

Funny thing how you first meet the woman that you marry. I first met the wife in a tunnel of love. She was digging it.

Les Dawson

My husband and I didn't sign a pre-nuptial agreement; we signed a mutual suicide pact.

Roseanne

Mary: John, once we had something that was pure and wonderful and good. What's happened to it?
John: You spent it all.

I'm Sorry, I'll Read That Again

My wife and I were married in a toilet; it was a marriage of convenience.

Tommy Cooper

He tricked me into marrying him. He told me he was pregnant.

Carol Leifer

I think men who have pierced ears are better prepared for marriage. They have experienced pain and bought jewellery.

Rita Rudner

I'd like to get married because I like the idea of a man being required by law to sleep with me every night.

Carrie Snow

Tonight, we'll be asking: "Should all married couples be frank and earnest, or should one of them be a woman?"

The Two Ronnies

Now, what is a wedding? Well, Webster's Dictionary describes a wedding as the process of removing weeds from one's garden.

Homer Simpson

If I get married again, I want a guy there with a drum to do rimshots during the vows.

Sam Kinison

Here in Hollywood you can actually get a marriage license printed on an Etch-A-Sketch.

Dennis Miller

Thelma Todd: But from the time he got the marriage license, I've led a dog's life.
Groucho: Are you sure he didn't get a dog's license?

The Marx Brothers (Monkey Business)

My wife is impossible. It's only safe to wake her from a distance, like Portugal.

Tim Allen

Coach: Norm, you're in here every night; doesn't your wife ever wonder where you're at?
Norm: Wonders. Doesn't care, but she wonders.

Cheers

Do you know what it means to come home at night to a woman who'll give you a little love, a little affection, a little tenderness? It means you're in the wrong house, that's what it means.

Henny Youngman

I had bad luck with both my wives. The first one left me and the second one didn't.

Bob Monkhouse

I take my wife everywhere, but she keeps finding her way back.

Henny Youngman

It was a mixed marriage. I'm human; he was a Klingon.

Carol Leifer

It's not easy to juggle a pregnant wife and a troubled child, but somehow I managed to fit in eight hours of TV a day.

Homer Simpson

My husband said he needed more space. So I locked him outside.

Roseanne

Ollie: Do you have to ask your wife everything?
Stan: Well, if I didn't ask her, I wouldn't know what she wanted me to do.

Laurel and Hardy

We always hold hands. If I let go, she shops.

Henny Youngman

Woody: Hey, Mr Peterson, there's a cold one waiting for you.
Norm: I know. If she calls, I'm not here.

Cheers

The other night I said to my wife Ruth: "Do you feel that the sex and excitement has gone out of our marriage?' Ruth said: "I'll discuss it with you during the next commercial."

Milton Berle

You want an amendment against same-sex marriage? Anyone who's ever been married knows it's always the same sex.

Robin Williams

Your marriage is in trouble if your wife says, "You're only interested in one thing," and you can't remember what it is.

Milton Berle

My psychiatrist said my wife and I should have sex every night. Now we'll never see each other!

Rodney Dangerfield

With men and women, does you think that men should marry only one woman? Does you believe in mahogany?

Ali G

Woman: Well, I was born Mary Patterson, but then I married and naturally took my husband's name. So now I'm Neil Patterson.

A Bit Of Fry and Laurie

MARTIAL ARTS

Karate is a form of martial arts in which people who have had years and years of training can, using only their hands and feet, make some of the worst movies in the history of the world.

Dave Barry

My other brother-in-law died. He was a karate expert, then joined the army. The first time he saluted, he killed himself.

Henny Youngman

MASOCHISM

I ache for the touch of your lips, dear
But much more for the touch of your whips, dear
You can raise welts
Like nobody else
As we dance to the Masochism Tango.

Tom Lehrer

MASSAGE

I went to a massage parlour. It was self-service.

Rodney Dangerfield

MASTURBATION

Steve: You know what they say; if music be the food of love, then masturbation is just a snack between meals.

Coupling

There's a fine line between masturbating while you look out a window, and masturbating while you're looking in a window.

Dave Attell

MATHS

Blackadder: Let's try again. If I have two beans and then I add two more beans, what does that make?
Baldrick: Umm... a very small casserole?

Blackadder

Ernie: I've got 23 A-levels, you know: 17 in mathematics, and another two, making 23.

Morecambe and Wise

Magnus Magnusson: A man has five children. Half of them are boys. Is that possible?
Sydney Bottocks: No.
Magnusson: Yes, the other half are also boys.

The Benny Hill Show

MATURITY

Basically, my wife was immature. I'd be at home, in the bath, and she'd walk right in whenever she felt like it... and sink my boats.

Woody Allen

I have a lot of growing up to do. I realised that the other day inside my fort.

Zach Galifianakis

Lister: I have a mind to fill your boots with runny porridge again. That'll teach you a lesson about maturity.

Red Dwarf

MEANNESS

And in a packed show tonight we'll be talking by long-distance phone to a Scotsman who found an Australian penny and emigrated.

The Two Ronnies

My Dad was a mean man; he hypnotised my mother not to order a starter!

Harry Hill

MEDICAL STUDENTS

Vyvyan: I've been down the morgue! I got a leg! I'm supposed to write an essay on it, but I think I'm just gonna stick it on the bonnet of my car!

The Young Ones

MEDICINE

I'm so full of penicillin at the moment, every time I sneeze I cure somebody.

Morecambe and Wise

Whitmore: Just a minute, Mrs Upjohn. That looks like a horse pill to me.
Dr. Hugo Hackenbush: Oh, you've taken them before.
Whitmore: Are you sure, Doctor? You haven't made a mistake?
Hackenbush: You have nothing to worry about. The last patient I gave one of those to won the Kentucky Derby.

The Marx Brothers (A Day At the Races)

MEDIEVAL LEARNING

Bedivere: ...and that, my liege, is how we know the Earth to be banana-shaped.
Arthur: This new learning amazes me, Sir Bedivere. Explain again how sheeps' bladders may be employed to prevent earthquakes.

Monty Python and the Holy Grail

MEETING

We looked at each other across a room full of people, our eyes met and she thought to herself, "One day, I'm going to divorce that man."

John Dowie

MEMENTOES

I hold your hand in mine, dear, I press it to my lips.
I take a healthy bite from your dainty fingertips.
My joy would be complete, dear, if you were only here,
But still I keep your hand
As a precious souvenir.

Tom Lehrer

MEMOIRS

Isn't this amazing? Clinton is getting eight million dollars for his memoir; Hillary got eight million for her memoir. That is sixteen million dollars for two people who for eight years couldn't remember anything.

Jay Leno

MEMORIALS

Blackadder: I think I'll write on my tombstone: "Here lies Edmund Blackadder, and he's bloody annoyed."

Blackadder

Eric: What would you like them to put on your tombstone?
Ernie: Nothing too grand, just: "Here lies the greatest writer what ever lived."

Morecambe and Wise

What do you get the man who has everything? Might I suggest a gravestone inscribed with the words, "So what?"

Simon Munnery

MEMORY

First you forget names. Then you forget faces. Next you forget to pull your zipper up and, finally, you forget to pull it down.

George Burns

Men forget everything; women remember everything. That's why men need instant replays in sports. They've already forgotten what happened.

Rita Rudner

I can remember when the air was clean and sex was dirty.

George Burns

MEN AND WOMEN

A man without a woman is like a neck without a pain.

W C Fields

A man's got to do what a man's got to do. A woman must do what he can't.

Rhonda Hansome

Doctor Crow: I am Doctor Crow. You are surprised?
Daphne Honeybutt: Yes, I am! I expected you to be a man... or a woman.

Carry On Spying

Guys are like dogs; they keep coming back. Ladies are like cats. Yell at a cat one time: they're gone.

Lenny Bruce

Men are superior to women; for one thing, they can urinate from a speeding car.

Will Durst

Men can read maps better than women, 'cos only the male mind could conceive of one inch equalling a hundred miles.

Roseanne

Men like cars; women like clothes. Women only like cars because they take them to clothes.

Rita Rudner

Stan: Men and women have different brains.
Dolly: Yes; it was in the Daily Mail. Women can't fold maps, and men can't get
    interested in headboards.

Dinnerladies

When women are depressed, they either eat or go shopping. Men invade
another country.

Elayne Boosler

Women; we're our own worst enemies a lot of the time. But I still blame men.

Janeane Garofalo

Women are cursed and men are the proof.

Roseanne

MEN AND WOMEN: MEN

I have this reputation as a man-hater and it's not true at all. I think men are
fantastic… as a concept.

Jo Brand

A man in the house is worth two in the street.

Mae West

All men are not homeless, but some men are home less than others.

Henny Youngman

And it's not easy being a man, you know. I had to get dressed today… and
there are other pressures.

Dylan Moran

Cliff: What a pathetic display. I'm ashamed God made me a man.
Carla: I don't think God's doing a lot of bragging either.

Cheers

Jeff: Do you know what would be the best way to wipe out all of human kind?
Make all women telepathic, because if they suddenly found out about the kind
of stuff that goes on in our heads, they'd kill us all on the spot.

Coupling

Deep down inside, men are biological creatures, like jellyfish or trees, only less likely to clean the bathroom.

Dave Barry

All human beings connect sex and love... except for men.

Roseanne

Don't let a man put anything over on you except an umbrella.

Mae West

I can eat a man, but I'm not sure of the fibre content.

Jenny Éclair

Give a man a free hand and he'll try to put it all over you.

Mae West

Men, on average, think about sex once every eight minutes. I make a point of thinking about sex every four seconds. This makes me 120 times more manly than the rest of you.

Simon Munnery

The difference between a man and a battery is that a battery has a positive side.

Jo Brand

To attract men, I wear a perfume called 'New Car Interior'.

Rita Rudner

To get a man's attention, just stand in front of the TV and don't move.

Tim Allen

MEN AND WOMEN: WOMEN

Men don't feel the urge to get married as quickly as women because their clothes all button and zip in the front. Women's dresses usually button and zip in the back. We need men emotionally and sexually, but we also need men to help us get dressed.

Rita Rudner

My sister was with two men in one night. She could hardly walk after that. Can you imagine? Two dinners!

Sarah Silverman

Women; you can't live with them, and you can't get them to dress up in a skimpy Nazi costume and beat you with a warm squash.

Emo Philips

Do you realise that Eve was the only woman who ever took a man's side?

Milton Berle

Girls are like pianos. When they're not upright, they're grand.

Benny Hill

I believe you should place a woman on a pedestal: high enough so you can look up her dress.

Steve Martin

I know I'm not gonna understand women. I will never understand how you can take boiling-hot wax, pour it on to your upper thigh, rip the hair out by the root – and still be afraid of a spider.

Jerry Seinfeld

I like a woman with a head on her shoulders. I hate necks.

Steve Martin

Women are like elephants. I like to watch them, but I wouldn't want to own one.

W C Fields

MESSIAH

Brian's mother: He's not the Messiah. He's a very naughty boy!

Monty Python's Life Of Brian

THE MIDDLE EAST

An Israeli man's life was saved when he was given a Palestinian man's heart in a heart transplant operation. The guy's doing fine, but the bad news is he can't stop throwing rocks at himself.

Jay Leno

MIDGETS

Bud: What's the idea of teaching midgets to wrestle?
Lou: They're for those small television sets.

Abbott and Costello

MILITARY

I entered the service after I graduated high school because the drop-outs already had the jobs.

Bill Cosby

Stephen Fry: What is attractive about the Costa Rican army?
Jo Brand: They have a pulse.

QI

We have women in the military, but they don't put us in the front lines. They don't know if we can fight; if we can kill. I think we can. All the general has to do is walk over to the women and say: "You see the enemy over there? They say you look fat in those uniforms."

Elayne Boosler

MIME

I used to be a narrator for bad mimes.

Steven Wright

The worst time to have a heart attack is during a game of charades.

Demetri Martin

159

MINIMUM WAGE

Minimum Wage is actually lower than it was in 1968. That's the same year George W Bush graduated from Yale, and that is unforgivable. And the wage thing is bad, too.

Bill Maher

MIRRORS

Bing... Bam... Boom: the sound three mirrors make when you look at them.

Drew Carey

The mirror above my bed reads: "Objects appear larger than they are."

Garry Shandling

The way a man looks at himself in a mirror will tell you if he can ever care about anyone else.

Rita Rudner

MISGIVINGS

Mrs Fussey: Joan may think you're a gentleman, but personally I've got sore misgivings.
Sid Boggle: You ought to put some talcum powder on them.

Carry On Camping

MISS UNIVERSE

Why is it that the winner of the Miss Universe contest always comes from Earth?

Rich Hall

MISSION IMPOSSIBLE

I saw a poster for Mission Impossible III the other day. I thought to myself: "It's not really impossible if he's already done it twice."

Mark Watson

MISTAKES

As long as the world is turning and spinning, we're gonna be dizzy and we're gonna make mistakes.

Mel Brooks

I've learned from my mistakes and I'm sure I can repeat them exactly.

Peter Cook

MONEY

Presenter: Good evening and welcome to Trying To Borrow A Fiver Off... Tonight I shall be Trying To Borrow A Fiver Off the conductor of the British Philharmonic Orchestra, Neville Anderson.

A Bit Of Fry and Laurie

Bart, with $10,000, we'd be millionaires! We could buy all kinds of useful things like... love!

Homer Simpson

Some people get so rich they lose all respect for humanity. That's how rich I want to be.

Rita Rudner

Bloodnok: This pound note. What colour was it?
Seagoon: Green.
Bloodnok: It's mine! Mine was green!

The Goon Show

Chico: One dollar and you'll remember me all your life.
Dr Hugo Hackenbush: That's the most nauseating proposition I ever had.

The Marx Brothers (A Day At the Races)

I'm the sort of person, if you lent me a fiver and never saw me again, it would be worth it.

Jerry Sadowitz

I love to go to Washington, if only to be nearer my money.

Bob Hope

I've got all the money I'll ever need… if I die by four o'clock this afternoon.

Henny Youngman

I have enough money to last me the rest of my life – unless I buy something.

Jackie Mason

Every morning I get up and look through the Forbes list of the richest people in America. If I'm not there, I go to work.

Robert Orben

I wasn't always rich. There was a time I didn't know where my next husband was coming from.

Mae West

Chico: Right now, I'd do anything for money. I'd kill somebody for money. I'd kill you for money… Ha ha ha! Ah, no. You're my friend. I'd kill you for nothing.

The Marx Brothers (The Cocoanuts)

Like a supermodel, I won't get out of bed for less than £20,000. Of course, it does mean I spend a lot of time in bed.

Clive Anderson

Money can't buy everything. That's what credit cards are for.

Ruby Wax

Money can't buy you happiness, but it does bring you a more pleasant form of misery.

Spike Milligan

Money can't buy you love, but it can get you some really good chocolate ginger biscuits.

Dylan Moran

Anybody who says money can't buy happiness doesn't know where to shop.

Jackie Gleason

Be careful of men who are bald and rich; the arrogance of 'rich' usually cancels out the nice of 'bald'.

Rita Rudner

My wife gets all the money I make. I just get an apple and clean clothes every morning.

Ray Romano

People say that money isn't the key to happiness, but I always figured if you have enough money, you can have a key made.

Joan Rivers

Strange things happen when you're in debt. Two weeks ago my car broke down and my phone got disconnected. I was one electric bill away from being Amish.

Tom Ryan

The only thing money gives you is the freedom of not worrying about money.

Johnny Carson

MONSTERS

Ronnie Barker: But now a sketch set in Frankenstein's castle in which I take the very important part of the monster.
Ronnie Corbett: And I make him put it back.

The Two Ronnies

MORMONS

I've got a mate who's a Mormon. He wrote the first ever Mormon musical, which is called Forty-seven Brides for Seven Brothers.

Frank Skinner

MORSE CODE

I would imagine that if you could understand Morse code, a tap-dancer would drive you crazy.

Mitch Hedberg

MOTHBALLS

I cannot smell mothballs because it's so difficult to get their little legs apart.

Steve Martin

MOTHERS-IN-LAW

I can always tell when the mother-in-law's coming to stay; the mice throw themselves on the traps.

Les Dawson

I told my mother-in-law that my house was her house. She said, "Get the hell off my property."

Joan Rivers

I wanted to do something nice, so I bought my mother-in-law a chair. Now they won't let me plug it in.

Henny Youngman

I took my mother-in-law to the Chamber of Horrors at Madame Tussaud's. One of the attendants said: "Keep her moving, sir; we're stocktaking."

Les Dawson

My mother-in-law broke up my marriage. My wife came home and found us in bed together.

Lenny Bruce

My wife said, "Can my mother come down for the weekend?" So I said, "Why?" And she said, "Well, she's been up on the roof two weeks already."

Bob Monkhouse

The wife's mother said: "When you're dead, I'll dance on your grave." I said, "Good, I'm being buried at sea."

Les Dawson

MOTIVATION

I was picked for my motivational skills. Everyone always says they have to work twice as hard when I'm around!

Homer Simpson

MOUNTAINS OUT OF MOLEHILLS

Diane: He's trying to make a mountain out of a molehill.
Carla: He wants you to wear a padded bra?

Cheers

MOUSTACHES

Captain Concoran: I said, one goes around with a black moustache.
Groucho: Well, you couldn't expect a moustache to go around by itself.

The Marx Brothers (Monkey Business)

MOVIES

One time I went to the drive-in in a cab. The movie cost me $95.

Steven Wright

The film industry is like Anne Robinson: always on the look-out for a new face.

Jack Dee

Andy Parsons (asked to come up with 'unlikely things to hear at the Oscars'):
Thank you. This'll be on eBay by tomorrow morning.

Mock the Week

MULTIPLE PERSONALITIES

Three years ago my sister was diagnosed with multiple personality syndrome – and there's nothing funny about that. Well, she called me the other day, and my caller ID exploded.

Zach Galifianakis

MURDER WEEKEND

One of my friends went on a murder weekend; now he's doing life for it.

Jack Dee

MUSEUMS

I went to the museum where they had all the heads and arms from the statues that are in all the other museums.

Steven Wright

MUSIC

I hate music, especially when it's played.

Jimmy Durante

I thought today I'd start by singing one of Irving Berlin's songs. But then I thought, "Why should I? He never sings any of mine."

Spike Milligan

I'll be very honest with you. I know two numbers. One is 'Clair de Lune' and the other one isn't. Do you have any preferences?

Victor Borge

It is sobering to consider that when Mozart was my age he had already been dead for a year.

Tom Lehrer

Andre Previn: You're playing all the wrong notes.
Eric: I'm playing all the right notes… but not necessarily in the right order.

Morecambe and Wise

(Showing his violin) It's a real Strad, you know. If it isn't, I'm out $110. The reason I got it so cheap is that it's one of the few Strads made in Japan.

Jack Benny

This concerto was written in four flats because Rachmaninoff had to move four times while he wrote it.

Victor Borge

Archie Bunker: Listen, Edith, I know you're singing, you know you're singing, but the neighbours may think I'm torturing you.

All In the Family

His vibrato sounded like he was driving a tractor over a ploughed field with weights tied to his scrotum.

Spike Milligan

Ali G (interviewing David and Victoria Beckham): So do you want Brooklyn to grow up to be a footballer like his dad, or a singer… like Mariah Carey?

Ali G

I take music pretty seriously. You see that scar on my wrist? You see that? You know where that's from? I heard the Bee Gees were getting back together again. I couldn't take it, OK?

Denis Leary

Why does Britney Spears sell so many millions of records? Because the public is horny and depressed.

Neil Hamburger

There's more evil in the charts than in an al Qaeda suggestion box.

Bill Bailey

Apparently, if you play country and Western music backwards, your lover returns, your dog comes back and you cease to be an alcoholic.

Linda Smith

Actually, listeners may be interested to learn that Colin spent many years working with Johnny Cash. Well, somebody had to empty those condom machines...

I'm Sorry I Haven't A Clue

Complete the lines from the following songs: 'I'm singing in the…' Well, EK of the Dwellings, Rotherhithe, your suggestion, while inaccurate, was interesting. I suppose you have to sing in there if the lock's broken.

Round the Horne

Go ahead and play the blues if it'll make you happy.

Homer Simpson

Students of music history may be interested to learn that Colin often used to produce Muddy Waters. And what a popular exam subject Colin is at the rare diseases unit…

I'm Sorry I Haven't A Clue

I do not have a single white note on my piano; my elephant smoked too much.

Victor Borge

I remixed a remix; it was back to normal.

Mitch Hedberg

Mick Shrimpton: As long as there's, you know, sex and drugs, I can do without the rock and roll.

Spinal Tap

Many people have asked me why there are three pedals in these grand pianos. Well, the pedal in the middle is there to separate the two other pedals.

Victor Borge

This is a wonderful orchestra. Every musician is an artist in her or his own right. It's only when we play together that we might have a little problem.

Victor Borge

Where would we be without good music? Here!

Les Dawson

The difference between a violin and a viola is that a viola burns longer.

Victor Borge

When she started to play, Steinway came down personally and rubbed his name off the piano.

Bob Hope

Would you like to hear the famous 'Polonaise in A Flat' by Chopin? Very well. Is there anyone here who can play it?

Victor Borge

MUSLIMS

Men who blow themselves up are promised 72 virgins in paradise. That's a high price to pay for a shag. In real life you'd be hard pushed to find one virgin. It begs the question: what on earth do they all look like? That's a lot of hairy women.

Shazia Mirza

You don't fuck with them double Muslims, 'cos they can't wait to get to Allah... and take eight or nine people with them.

Richard Pryor

MUZAK

I worry that the person who thought up muzak may be thinking up something else.

Lily Tomlin

NAMES

Alice: You can call me Alice, 'cos that's my name.

The Vicar of Dibley

My name's Norman Lovett. That's my real name. And if I had a pound for every time someone's said, "Lovett? I bet you do," I'd have about six or seven pounds by now.

Norman Lovett

Pontius Pilate: I will not have my fwiends widiculed by the common soldiewy. Anybody else feel like a little... giggle... when I mention my fwiend... Biggus... Dickus?

Monty Python's Life of Brian

Some names have class connotations. I was born on a council estate, but once I'd been called Jeremy, we had to move.

Jeremy Hardy

Wanda: And when he heard your daughter's name was Portia...
Archie: Yes?
Wanda: He said, "Why did they name her after a car?"

A Fish Called Wanda

I used to be Snow White, but I drifted.

Mae West

People get burned out in big families. You can even see it in the naming of children, like, the first kid: "You were named after Grandma." The seventh kid: "You were named after a sandwich I had. Now get your brother, Reuben."

Jim Gaffigan

NATURAL DISASTERS

They say animal behaviour can warn you when an earthquake is coming. Like, the night before that last earthquake hit, our family dog took the car keys and drove to Arizona.

Bob Hope

NEEDING TO TALK

George: She calls me up at my office. She says, "We have to talk."
Jerry: Uh – the four worst words in the English language.
George: That, or, "Whose bra is this?"

Seinfeld

If your wife says to you, "We need to talk," horse shit. Start a fire in your house, it's easier to deal with. Cause when your wife says to you, "We need to talk" it does not mean we need to talk, it means you need to sit there and listen while I tell you all the ways you've been fuckin' up! That's what that means. You ain't never gonna hear a man say, "We need to talk." ...Unless...He caught a disease while he was out fishing..

Rodney Carrington

NEIGHBOURS

Frankie Boyle (asked to come up with 'The worst thing your new neighbour could say'): What day do the bins go out round here? My wife's body is starting to stink!

Mock the Week

Hugh Dennis (answering the same question): My wife breeds Rottweilers, my kids are in a brass band, and I'm a paedophile.

Mock the Week

NEIL KINNOCK

I think Neil Kinnock's got a certain amount of street credibility. From a certain angle he looks like a Belisha beacon.

Jerry Sadowitz

NERVES

Hanging Lady: Nervous?
Ted Striker: Yes.
Hanging Lady: First time?
Ted Striker: No, I've been nervous lots of times.

Airplane!

NEW YORK

Anytime four New Yorkers get into a cab together without arguing, a bank robbery has just taken place.

Johnny Carson

New York is an exciting town where something's happening all the time, most unsolved.

Johnny Carson

New York now leads the world's great cities in the number of people around whom you shouldn't make a sudden move.

David Letterman

New York. When civilization falls apart, remember – we were way ahead of you.

David Letterman

New York's such a wonderful city. Although I was at the library today. The guys are very rude. I said, 'I'd like a card.' He says, 'You have to prove you're a citizen of New York.' So I stabbed him.

Emo Philips

Tip to out-of-town visitors: If you buy something here in New York and want to have it shipped home, be suspicious if the clerk tells you they don't need your name and address.

David Letterman

NEWS HEADLINES

Chris Morris: Branson's clockwork dog crosses Atlantic floor.

The Day Today

Chris Morris: Girl made of paint wins by-election.

The Day Today

Chris Morris: And where now for man raised by puffins?

The Day Today

Chris Morris: The Libyan leader Colonel Gadaffi has plunged southern Europe into crisis by kidnapping Crete and towing it to a secret location off the Libyan coast.

The Day Today

NIGHT CAPS

Jane Spencer: Would you like a nightcap?
Frank: No, thank you, I don't wear them.

The Naked Gun

NIGHT IN

Rimmer: Kryten, unpack Rachel and get out the puncture repair kit. I'm alive!

Red Dwarf

NOISE

If you must make a noise, make it quietly.

Laurel and Hardy

Marty DiBergi: That night, I heard a band that, for me, redefined the word "rock and roll". I remember being knocked out by their... their exuberance, their raw power – and their punctuality. That band was Britain's now-legendary Spinal Tap. Seventeen years and fifteen albums later, Spinal Tap is still going strong. And they've earned a distinguished place in rock history as one of England's loudest bands.

Spinal Tap

NORTH

Continuity announcer: I'd like to apologise to viewers in the North. It must be awful for them.

Victoria Wood: As Seen On TV

NOSES

Our nose is badly designed; the snot falls out. If there's going to be stuff in your nose, it shouldn't be runny and able to dribble out. Really, our nose should be on the other way up: but then, when you sneezed, your hair would get two side partings and your eyes'd be full of snot. Also, you'd drown when it rained. Isn't life complicated?

Billy Connolly

NOT WHAT I DO

It's not what I do but how I do it. It's not what I say but how I say it. And how I look when I'm saying and doing it.

Mae West

173

NOTTINGHAM

Nottingham is a fine city with a fascinating history. It's well documented in official records that the city's original name was 'Snottingham', or 'Home of Snots', but when the Normans came, they couldn't pronounce the letter 'S', so decreed the town be called 'Nottingham' or 'Home of Notts'. It's easy to understand why this change was resisted so fiercely by the people of Scunthorpe.

I'm Sorry I Haven't A Clue

NUCLEAR ATTACK

We shall receive four minutes' warning of any impending nuclear attack. Some people have said, "Oh, my goodness me: four minutes? That's not a very long time!" Well, I would remind those doubters that some people in this great country of ours can run a mile in four minutes.

Peter Cook (Beyond the Fringe)

You can't say you wouldn't want to be bombed in a nuclear attack, if you've never been bombed. You might quite like it. Lots of chaps in the last war quite took to it. Said it gave them a chance to see just what sort of stuff they were made of.

Radio Active

NUCLEAR REACTORS

It's been 18 years since the Chernobyl disaster. Is it just me who's surprised – no superheroes?

Jimmy Carr

You know, boys, a nuclear reactor is a lot like a woman. You just have to read the manual and press the right buttons.

Homer Simpson

NUDITY

I'm an intensely shy and vulnerable woman. My husband Norm has never seen me naked. Nor has he ever expressed the least desire to do so.

Dame Edna Everage

'm not comfortable with my own body. I shower with my clothes on.

Conan O'Brien

Joey: Hey, Mon, I got a question for you.
Monica: Okay, for the bizillionth time, yes, I see other women in the shower at the gym, and no, I don't look.

Friends

Nicholas Parsons: Are Thames executives against attractive nude women?
Fred Scuttle: Not as often as they'd like to be!

The Benny Hill Show

The search for the man who terrorises nudist camps with a bacon slicer goes on. Inspector Lemuel Jones had a tip-off this morning, but hopes to be back on duty tomorrow.

The Two Ronnies

OBITUARIES

When I die, if the word 'thong' appears in the first or second sentence of my obituary, I've screwed up.

Albert Brooks

OIL

I've got a friend who's in oil. He's in oil in a small way. He's a sardine.

Clive Anderson

ON YOUR TOES

Frank Drebin: Like a midget at a urinal, I'd have to be on my toes.

The Naked Gun

OPEN MIND

Now there's a man with an open mind; you can feel the breeze from here!

Groucho Marx

OPENING A DOOR

Bluebottle: Eccles, why do you not open the door?
Eccles: Okay, I'll – how do you open a door?
Bluebottle: You turn the knob on your side.
Eccles: I haven't got a knob on my side!

The Last Goon Show of A

OPERA

Henry McGee: What is the name of this opera you're presenting?
Chow Mein: Little white buttercup.
McGee: The opera is called Little White Buttercup?
Chow Mein: No, she a little white buttercup.
McGee: Oh, she's called Little White Buttercup?
Chow Mein: No, I say to her, "You lift your right buttock up."

The Benny Hill Sho

OPINIONS

People have different opinions on things. For example: to me, my girlfriend is the most wonderful, beautiful person in the world. That's to me: but to my wife…

Jackie Maso

OPTICIANS AND EYESIGHT

All the other kids used to call me Four Eyes. I wouldn't mind, but I didn't wear glasses.

John Dow

I wear glasses myself: as an affectation, as a badge of high intellect and to see with.

Simon Munne

My local optician got busted. Turns out all his eye charts were out of focus.

Jack De

I have such poor vision I can date anybody.

Garry Shandling

I got contact lenses recently, but I only need them when I read, so I got flip-ups.

Steven Wright

I have bad eyesight. When I go to the optician's he points to the chart, reads them out himself and says, "True or false"?

Woody Allen

Willium: I must admit, me eyes ain't what they used to be.
Seagoon: No?
Willium: No, they used to be me ears.

The Goon Show

ORANGE ORDER

Ali G: Do you have music at this march?
George Paton (Northern Ireland Orange Lodge Grandmaster): Oh, yes, yes, lots of music, the whole works.
Ali G: For real. Do you have drums?
Paton: Drums, yes.
Ali G: And is you like knocking out a drum and bass thing or is it more kind of speed garage that you is knocking out?
Paton: It's all there; different drummers have their own rhythms; it's an individual thing.
Ali G: Do you not think though, me just not giving advice but me sayin' from me own experience, sometimes it's good to back up the drums with a bit of human beatbox?

Ali G

ORIGINAL SIN

"Bless me, Father, for I have sinned. I did an original sin. I poked a badger with a spoon."
"Say five Hail Marys and six Hello Dollys!"

Eddie Izzard

OSMONDS

In the legal proceedings surrounding the Osmonds' split-up, Donny Osmond has been awarded custody of the teeth.

Not the Nine O'Clock News

OUTDOORS

I hate the outdoors. To me, the outdoors is where the car is.

Will Durst

OZONE HOLE

It's absolutely stupid that we live without an ozone layer. We have men, we've got rockets, we've got saran wrap – FIX IT!

Lewis Black

The ozone hole over the Antarctic may soon set the record as being the world's biggest. This is the first year that the world's biggest hole will not be a head of state.

Rick Mercer

PALAEONTOLOGY

Joey: What the hell does a palaeontologist need a beeper for?
Monica: Is it like for dinosaur emergencies? "Help, come quick, they're still extinct."

Friends

PANIC

Bernard: You mean help him overcome his panic?
Sir Humphrey: No, no, no, no, no. We must let him panic. Politicians like to panic. They need activity. It's their substitute for achievement.

Yes, Minister

PARENTS

I said, "Darling, I'll be a great father. I'll be there at the birth and everything."
She said, "John, I don't want you there at the conception."

John Dowie

Well, it's 1am. Better go home and spend some quality time with the kids.

Homer Simpson

Ali G: So tell me, is your little boy starting to put whole sentences together?
Victoria Beckham: He's saying little bits and pieces, yeah.
Ali G: And what about Brooklyn?

Ali G

Chandler: If I turn into my parents, I'll either be an alcoholic blonde chasing after
20-year-old boys, or... I'll end up like my mom.

Friends

Frasier: If it wasn't biologically impossible, I'd swear that Dad was dropped in a
basket on our doorstep.

Frasier

I was raised by just my mom. See, my father died when I was eight years old. At
least, that's what he told us in the letter.

Drew Carey

The remarkable thing about my mother is that for 30 years she served us
nothing but leftovers. The original meal has never been found.

Calvin Trillin

The other night I told my kid, "Some day, you'll have children of your own." He
said, "So will you."

Rodney Dangerfield

I had to tell my dad I wasn't going to be a footballer. I told him I was doing a
degree in performing arts instead. He said, "Why are you doing this to me?"
I said, "I don't know... but I can show you through expressive dance."

Alan Carr

PARTIES

I once went to one of those parties where everyone throws their car keys into the middle of the room... I don't know who got my moped, but I drove that Peugeot for years.

Victoria Wood: As Seen On TV

The producer's parties can get a bit dreary. I remember the last one: a lightbulb blew out and we were still laughing about it two hours later.

Ronnie Corbett

When I went to college, my parents threw a going-away party for me, according to the letter.

Emo Philips

PARTIONING YOUR HOUSE

Harold (trying to get Albert to change the channel of the TV in the house they have partitioned so they can live separately): We had an agreement; we shook hands. I have got the law of contract on my side.
Albert: I have the knobs on my side.

Steptoe and Son

PATTER OF LITTLE FEET

Ah, the patter of little feet around the house. There's nothing like having a midget for a butler.

W C Fields

We've begun to long for the pitter-patter of little feet – so we bought a dog. Well, it's cheaper, and you get more feet.

Rita Rudner

PENISES

(On the tendency of black men to hold their crotches): White people be going, "Why do you hold your things?" "'Cos you took everything else!"

Richard Pryor

Annie: And then she mentioned penis envy. Do you know about that?
Alvy Singer: Me? I'm... I'm one of the few males who suffers from that.

Annie Hall

I once made love to a female clown. It was weird, because she twisted my penis into a poodle.

Dan Whitney

I went to my doctor and told him: "My penis is burning." He said, "That means somebody's talking about it."

Garry Shandling

In Cambodia, a woman tried to cut off her husband's penis and he ended up receiving 25 stitches. Not surprisingly, the man told his buddies he needed 50 stitches.

Conan O'Brien

Why did God give Motlëy Crüe such abnormally large penises? So that they'd be better equipped at dealing with the pain of life.

Neil Hamburger

I hate those e-mails where they try to sell you penis enhancers. I got ten just the other day: eight of them from my girlfriend. It's the two from my mum that really hurt.

Jimmy Carr

PEOPLE

Elaine: Ugh, I hate people.
Jerry: Yeah, they're the worst.

Seinfeld

Apparently you can tell a lot about people from what they're like.

Harry Hill

Cheryl: I thought you didn't like talking to people.
Larry: I don't like talking to... to people I KNOW, but strangers I have no
    problem with.

Curb Your Enthusiasm

Archie Bunker: I got nothin' against mankind. It's people I can't stand.

All In the Family

I think I'm a pretty good judge of people, which is why I hate most of them.

Roseanne

Ninety-eight per cent of the adults in this country are decent, hardworking, honest Americans. It's the other lousy two per cent that get all the publicity, but then, we elected them.

Lily Tomlin

There are two types of people in this world: those who live in the cities – or 'citizens', as I call them – and those who live in the countryside... who shall remain nameless.

Simon Munnery

PERSONALISED NUMBERPLATES

Del: Here, Boycie, you know this car's a GTI? If you rearrange the letters, then you got yourself a personalised numberplate!

Only Fools And Horses

PERSPECTIVE

Ted (showing Dougal plastic cows – the sort you'd get with a toy farm set): OK, one last time. These are small, and the ones out there (pointing out of the window) are far away...

Father Ted

PERVERSION

Ross: Rachel won't talk to me. She won't even let me in the apartment.
Phoebe: Hmmm, I wonder why, pervert?
Ross: I'm not a pervert.
Phoebe: Please! That's the pervert motto. They have you raise your right hand, put your left hand in your pants and say that.

Friends

PETER PAN

J M Barrie spent some time in Nottingham, where he was inspired to write Peter Pan after spotting an urchin running in the street. What a one-in-a-million chance that one should have escaped from the Marine Biology Aquarium that very day.

I'm Sorry I Haven't A Clue

PETS

I feel sad for people who have to buy animals to keep them company. I hope I never get to the stage where I have to go to a pet shop to buy my friends.

Jack Dee

PHILADELPHIA

I once spent a year in Philadelphia; I think it was on a Sunday.

W C Fields

PHONE VOTES

I was watching the news and they had one of those polls where you call in and vote on an issue. You can call in "Yes," "No," or "Undecided," and "Undecided" caught six per cent of the vote. This means that there are people in this country who'll take time and spend money to call and tell us they can't make up their mind.

Dennis Regan

PHONES

My phone number is 17. I got one of the early ones.

George Carlin

I tried phone sex and it gave me an ear infection.

Richard Lewis

Nana: I wanted to do one of those Friends and Family but I couldn't make up the numbers. Most of 'em were dead.

The Royle Family

Now we have hands-free phones, so you can focus on the thing you're really supposed to be doing. Chances are, if you need both of your hands to do something, your brain should be in on it too.

Ellen DeGeneres

So I got home, and the phone was ringing. I picked it up, and said, "Who's speaking, please?" and a voice said, "You are."

Tim Vine

PHOTOS

If you look like your passport photograph, in all probability you need the holiday.

Earl Wilson

PILGRIM FATHERS

Celebrate the Pilgrims? Fuck them. What a bunch of morons! You ever look at them? They had belts on their hats. I would've loved to have been at that meeting. How stupid were these people? "Our hats keep blowing off in the wind. Let's put belts on them." "Good thinking, Jacob!"

Jeremy Hotz

PLANES AND FLYING

If God had intended us to fly, He'd have sent us tickets.

Mel Brooks

All it takes to fly is to hurl yourself at the ground... and miss.

The Hitchhiker's Guide To the Galaxy

Lieutenant Flashheart: You should treat your aircraft like you treat your woman.
Blackadder: So you should take your plane out to dinner and a movie?
Flashheart: No, get in her five times a day and take her to heaven and back!

Blackadder

At the airport, they asked me if anybody I didn't know gave me anything. Even the people I know don't give me anything.

George Wallace

Elaine Dickinson (reassuring the passengers after a slight problem has occurred during the flight): There's no reason to become alarmed, and we hope you'll enjoy the rest of your flight. By the way, is there anyone on board who knows how to fly a plane?

Airplane!

I knew I'd chosen the wrong airline when the flight attendant warned us to keep our hands and arms inside the aircraft while it was in motion. The airsick bag was printed with the Lord's Prayer.

Les Dawson

If airline travel is so safe, how come the stewardesses sit right next to the emergency exits?

Johnny Carson

The odds against there being a bomb on a plane are a million to one, and against two bombs a million times a million to one. Next time you fly, cut the odds and take a bomb.

The Benny Hill Show

When I'm on a plane, I can never get my seat to recline more than a couple of centimetres, but the guy in front of me – his seat comes back far enough for me to do dental work on him.

Ellen DeGeneres

PLASTIC

There's so much plastic in this culture that vinyl leopard skin is becoming an endangered synthetic.

Lily Tomlin

PLAYING WITH YOUR NAVEL

My mom got me back one day. I was playing with my navel. My mom said, "All right. You playing with your navel, pretty soon you gonna break it wide open. The air's going to come right out of your body. You'll fly around the room backwards for thirty seconds, land, you'll be flat as a piece of paper: nothing but your little eyes bugging out.

Bill Cosby

185

PLUMBERS

Samantha has to nip off now, as her plumber is sending round the man who does the annual safety test on her gas boiler, which always gives her great peace of mind. She says it's good to feel the plumber's tester calls at regular intervals.

I'm Sorry I Haven't A Clue

POETRY

Hancock: "I wish I were a chestnut tree, a-nourished by the sun, with twigs and leaves and branches, and conkers by the ton." Follow that! Robert Browning? I wouldn't give him houseroom.

Hancock's Half Hour

POLICE

Denver Mills: I'd like to welcome you all to the Annual Police Dinner. My name is Denver Mills and I am a former Olympic silver medallist. When I think about it, being an Olympic runner is a lot like being a police officer; we both spend most of our running chasing after black guys, but the difference is I actually beat some of mine, not just BEAT them like you do.

Little Britain

Frank: It's true what they say, cops and women don't mix. It's like eating a spoonful of Drano. Sure, it'll clean you out, but it'll leave you hollow inside.

The Naked Gun

Policemen are numbered in case they get lost.

Spike Milligan

POLITICAL CORRECTNESS

Brent: Look at this; "Dutch girls must be punished for having big boobs." Now, you do not punish a girl, Dutch or otherwise, for having big boobs.
Gareth: If anything, they should be rewarded.
Brent: No, they should be equal.

The Office

I'm sick and tired of people coming up to me and saying, "Paul, you're a sexist."
I'm not a sexist. I'm a radical feminist. I think you've got to be these days if you
want to get your end away.

Paul Calf (Steve Coogan)

POLITICS

Seeing Arnold's performance as Governor has really changed my mind about
actors becoming politicians. I don't know what I'm going to do with my box of
"Van Damme in '08" T-shirts.

John MacLain

Democracy means that anyone can grow up to be president and anyone who
doesn't grow up can be vice-president.

Johnny Carson

I said, "I'm sorry." I said, "I don't take part. I'm not interested. I don't take part in
any organised political bodies," I said. "I'm a Liberal."

Frankie Howerd

If presidents can't do it to their wives, they do it to their country.

Mel Brooks

If women ran the world, there would be no wars: just intense negotiations every
28 days.

Robin Williams

In case you think I'm talking about politics, don't worry, because I'm a pathetic
girlie and I don't know anything about it. Civil war in Yugoslavia? That's not going
to get the beds made and the washing-up done.

Jo Brand

In my lifetime, we've gone from Eisenhower to George W Bush. We've gone
from John F Kennedy to Al Gore. If this is evolution, I believe that in 12 years,
we'll be voting for plants.

Lewis Black

In the last election a total of £75,000 was spent upgrading John Prescott's battle-bus – by adding a waterbed, mirrors on the ceiling and strengthening the rear suspension.

Have I Got News For You

In Washington, a man gets up to speak and doesn't say a thing, and the other men disagree with him for three hours.

Milton Berle

Liberals feel unworthy of their possessions. Conservatives feel they deserve everything they've stolen.

Mort Sahl

Mrs Teal: Oh, are you standing in the by-election, Daffyd?
Daffyd: It's not just a bi-election; it's for gays and straights too!

Little Britain

My friends, in the light of present-day developments, let me say right away that I do not regard existing conditions likely.

Peter Sellers (Party Political Speech)

One day the don't-knows will get in and then where will we be?

Spike Milligan

Rick: Neil, the bathroom's free – unlike the country under the Thatcherite junta.

The Young Ones

Ronald Reagan won the election because he ran against Jimmy Carter. Had Reagan run unopposed, he would have lost.

Mort Sahl

The only reason I'm not running for president is that I'm afraid no woman will come forward and say she's slept with me.

Garry Shandling

The Weakest Link… is a fascinating programme. They ask a bunch of people questions and they keep getting rid of the dumbest person, so just the smartest person is left. It's kind of the opposite way we elect a president.

Jay Leno

Too bad all the people who know how to run this country are busy driving taxis and cutting hair.

George Burns

Washington couldn't tell a lie, Nixon couldn't tell the truth and Reagan couldn't tell the difference.

Mort Sahl

Hugh Dennis (asked to come up with 'ways not to start a party political broadcast'): My fellow-paedophiles...

Mock the Week

When I'm in power, here's how I'm gonna put the country back on its feet. I'm going to put sterilising agents in the following products: Sunny Delight, Mountain Dew and Thick-Crust Pizza.

Adam Carolla

You'll notice that Nancy Reagan never drinks water when Ronnie speaks.

Robin Williams

POP-UP BOOKS

A bit of advice: never read a pop-up book about giraffes.

Sean Lock

POPE

I think it'd be great if you had a kid that ended up being Pope. That would be the ultimate bragging rights. "Oh, your son's a doctor? Yeah, ours is Pope. They have a house? He has his own city... it's in Europe."

Jim Gaffigan

PORNOGRAPHY

That is one of my big fears in life: that I'm gonna die, you know, and my parents are gonna come to clean out my apartment, find that porno wing I've been adding on to for years. There'll be two funerals that day.

Bill Hicks

Eric: Lord Longford asked me what to do about the Pornography Bill. I told him straight. I said, "Pay it!"

Morecambe and Wise

(On the debate about what constitutes art and what pornography) If you can't masturbate to it, it's art.

Sean Lock

Ali G (on film classification): Do you not think that the category "18" is too vague? Do you not think that you should 'ave a category that guarantees you muff?

Ali G

I thought Deep Throat was a movie about a giraffe.

Bob Hope

If you were a lad, you couldn't watch a bit o' blue in t'middle of night, 'cos everybody could hear it fast-forwardin' about three streets away.

Peter Kay

My boyfriend used to say, "I read Playboy for the articles." Right, and I go to shopping malls for the music.

Rita Rudner

Why do people say that Playboy causes sexual thoughts? No, ladies and gentlemen, let me clear up once and for all what causes sexual thoughts: having a dick... or, for women, whatever ya got.

Bill Hicks

POSTCARDS

Whenever I'm out of town for at least a week, I feel like I should write a postcard or something, but you can be a genius, you try and write a postcard, you come across like a moron anyway: "This city's got big buildings, I like food, 'bye."

Jim Gaffigan

POVERTY

I can't forget the poverty-stricken days of my youth. I never had any shoes.
My father used to black my feet and lace my toes up.

Les Dawson

Blackadder: I'm as poor as a church mouse that's just had an enormous tax bill
on the very day his wife ran off with another mouse, taking all the cheese.

Blackadder

Christmases were terrible. Not like nowadays, when kids get everything. My
sister got a miniature set of perfumes called Ample. It was tiny, but even I could
see where my dad had scraped off the 'S' ...

Stephen K Amos

I used to sell furniture for a living. Unfortunately it was my own.

Les Dawson

Poor? I couldn't afford the doctor's bill. You're looking at the only man in the
world who's had his appendix taken out and put back in again.

Morecambe and Wise

We were kind of poor and my mother hated to spend a nickel on herself, so she
bought most of her things in an army surplus store. She was the only woman in
Cleveland wearing khaki lipstick.

Bob Hope

We were so poor that we couldn't afford a turkey. We gave the budgie chest
expanders. It was five-a-side to a cracker.

Les Dawson

PREGNANCY

"Do you mind if I sit down, 'cos I'm pregnant?" a woman said. I said in reply,
"You don't look it. How long have you been pregnant?" She said, "Only ten
minutes – but doesn't it make you feel tired?"

Max Miller

191

I looked up the symptoms of pregnancy – moody, irritable, big bosoms.
I've obviously been pregnant for 36 years.

Victoria Wood: As Seen On TV

PREJUDICE

I am free of all prejudices. I hate everyone equally.

W C Fields

A black C student can't do shit with his life. A black C student can't be a
manager at Burger King. Meanwhile a white C student just happens to be the
President of the United States.

Chris Rock

I'm really enjoying the new Martin Luther King Jr stamp; just think about all those
white bigots, licking the backside of a black man.

Dick Gregory

Jews were always discriminated against and persecuted and they found the
best way to survive was to become a doctor. No one's going to persecute a
doctor. Who's going to walk into a doctor's office and say, "My foot hurts… you
Jew bastard!"

Jackie Mason

PREMATURE EJACULATION

I went to a meeting for premature ejaculators. I left early.

Jack Benny

Recent surveys show three out of ten men have a problem with premature
ejaculation. The rest just didn't really think it was a problem!

Frankie Boyle

PRESENTS

I wrapped my Christmas presents early this year, but I used the wrong paper.
See, the paper I used said, "Happy Birthday" on it. I didn't want to waste it,
so I just wrote "Jesus" on it.

Demetri Martin

Sean Lock: I got the worst Christmas present ever, ever in my life. My sister gave me a "Grow Your Own Loofah" kit. It was a clay pot, a bag of earth and five seeds. And I think the clay pot hit her hardest.

QI

PRISON

He was doing a sentence – triple life! How do you do triple life? I mean if he die and then come back he has to go back to the penitentiary? "Fuck kindergarten, get your little ass back to the penitentiary!"

Richard Pryor

PROBLEMS

Blackadder: We're in a sticky situation all right. This is the stickiest situation since Sticky the stick insect got caught on a sticky bun.

Blackadder

I have yet to see any problem, however complicated, which, when you looked at it in the right way, did not become still more complicated.

Paul Anderson

Personally, I always tell my troubles to my enemies. They're the only ones who really want to hear them.

Robert Orben

The toughest time in anyone's life is when you have to kill a loved one just because they're the devil.

Emo Philips

PROBLEMS SPEAKING WORMS

Mrs Spooner: Do you feel like some breakfast?
The Reverend Spooner: Indood I dee! A suggestion to warm the hartles of my – cockles of my heart. I rather fancy some hot toatered bust, a rasher of strakey beacon and some of that cereal that goes pap, snockle and crap!

The Two Ronnies

PROCRASTINATION

If procrastination was an Olympic event, I wouldn't even turn up.

David O'Doherty

PROMISE AUCTIONS

Richard Lewis: Can't we have lunch or something and discuss this?
Larry: I can't.
Lewis: Why not?
Larry: I've been auctioned off for some charity.
Lewis: What is this, Roots?

Curb Your Enthusiasm

PROPOSALS

Dr Hugo Hackenbush: Emily, I have a confession to make. I really am a horse doctor, but marry me, and I'll never look at another horse.

The Marx Brothers (A Day At the Races)

Hugh: I'm afraid I was very much the traditionalist. I went down on one knee and dictated a proposal which my secretary faxed over straightaway.

A Bit Of Fry and Laurie

Firefly: Will you marry me? Did he leave you any money? Answer the second question first.

The Marx Brothers (Duck Soup)

PROSTATE

My husband Norm hasn't been a well man. I've had his prostate hanging over my head for many years.

Dame Edna Everage

PROSTITUTION

A hooker told me, "Not on the first date."

Rodney Dangerfield

You wanna hear my personal opinion on prostitution? If men knew how to do it, they wouldn't have to pay for it.

Roseanne

PROTESTS

I thought it was great when those women went down the mine recently and did that protest. Bet they left it nice and tidy, didn't they?

Jo Brand

PROXIMITY

If I held you any closer I'd be on the other side of you.

Groucho Marx

PSYCHICS

If it's the Psychic Network, why do they need a phone number?

Robin Williams

Mrs Slocombe: You know, animals are very psychic. I mean, the least sign of danger and my pussy's hair stands on end.

Are You Being Served?

PSYCHOANALYSIS

Miles (after waking up in the distant future): I haven't seen my analyst in 200 years. He was a strict Freudian. If I'd been going all this time, I'd probably almost be cured by now.

Sleeper

PUBLIC SCHOOL

It's the Eton housemaster who's invented a board game based on life at the famous public school. He says if it's a success, he'll bring out a state school version in which, if you throw three double sixes in a row, you still don't get anywhere.

Have I Got News For You

PUBLIC TRANSPORT

LA bus drivers are striking. They want a big raise, and they want it in exact change.

Jay Leno

PURPOSE

The Book: There is a theory which states that if anybody ever discovers exactly what the Universe is for and why it is here, it will instantly disappear and be replaced by something even more bizarre and inexplicable. There is another theory which states that this has already happened.

The Hitchhiker's Guide To the Galaxy

QUALIFICATIONS

Lister: You sign all your official letters "Arnold Rimmer BSc" and the BSc stands for "Bronze Swimming Certificate".

Red Dwarf

QUESTS

Colonel: Tell me, Captain, what are you going to look for?
Captain Cleese: Something all men desire.
Colonel: King Solomon's Mine?
Captain Cleese: That's all right, you can have him.

I'm Sorry, I'll Read That Again

RACIAL STEREOTYPES

I'm Scottish and Jewish: two racial stereotypes for the price of one.

Arnold Brown

RADIO

Ah, it's marvellous to be able to converse with people all over the world: people different to yourself, with something new to say. It broadens your outlook; increases your knowledge of things. I bet there's not many people round here who know it's not raining in Tokyo.

Tony Hancock (The Radio Ham)

Radio: that wonderful invention by which I can reach millions of people who fortunately can't reach me.

Milton Berle

REALITY

I can take reality in small doses, but not as a lifestyle.

Lily Tomlin

Reality is a crutch for people who can't handle drugs.

Lily Tomlin

Reality is nothing but a collective hunch.

Lily Tomlin

REALITY TELEVISION

I don't like this reality television, I have to be honest. I think real people should not be on television. It's for special people like us. People who have trained and studied to appear to be real.

Garry Shandling

RECORD-BREAKERS

In New York, David Blaine failed to break the world record for holding his breath underwater… David Blaine narrowly failed to beat the previous world record, which was set by a man who held his breath for almost nine minutes, after following John Prescott into the lavatory at the House of Commons.

Have I Got News For You

RECYCLING

"How's the wife?" "Oh, she's dead." "What?" "I murdered her this morning." "You're kidding me on!" "No. I'll show you, if you like." So he goes away up to his tenement building, through the close and there's a big mound of earth there and, sure enough, there's a bum sticking out. He says, "Is that her?" He says, "Aye." He says, "Why'd you leave her bum sticking out? He says, "I need somewhere to park my bike."

Billy Connolly

REDHEADS

She was a redhead: no hair, just a red head.

Les Dawson

REFLEXES

I have bad reflexes, and I can't fight. I was once run over by a car with a flat tyre, being pushed by two guys.

Woody Allen

REFUSE

My plumbing is all screwed up, because it turns out I do not own a garbage disposal.

Demetri Martin

REFUSE COLLECTION

She ran after the garbage truck, yelling, "Am I too late for the garbage?" "No, jump in!"

Henny Youngman

REINCARNATION

I spend money with reckless abandon. I spent $5,000 on a seminar about reincarnation. I got to thinking, "What the hell? You only live once."

Ronnie Shakes

RELATIONSHIPS

I know what men want. Men want to be really, really close to someone who will leave them alone.

Elayne Boosler

RELIEF

For fast-acting relief, try slowing down.

Lily Tomlin

RELIGION

A good sermon should have a good beginning and a good ending, and they should be as close together as possible.

George Burns

A lot of people are giving out about that film The Passion of the Christ saying it's anti-Semitic; saying it makes out it was the Jews that killed Christ. Well? It wasn't the Mexicans!

Tommy Tiernan

After the show, these three rednecks came up to me. "Hey, buddy! We're Christians and we didn't like what you said." I said, "Then forgive me." Later on, when I was hanging from the tree…

Bill Hicks

All things foul and ugly
All creatures short and squat
Putrid, foul and gangrenous
The Lord God made the lot,

Monty Python's Contractual Obligation Record

Bart: What religion are you?
Homer: You know, the one with all the well-meaning rules that don't work out in
  real life… uh… Christianity.

The Simpsons

Born again? No, I'm not. Excuse me for getting it right the first time.

Dennis Miller

David Horton: Dibley can't afford a new window.
Geraldine: Wait a minute! "Can't" isn't in the Christian vocabulary!
Owen: Yes, it is! You can't commit adultery; you can't steal…
Jim: You can't even covet your neighbour's ass… even if it is very alluring!

The Vicar of Dibley

Every day people are straying away from the church and going back to God.

Lenny Bruce

> Geraldine: And where was Jesus born?
> Child: In Dunstable.
> Geraldine: Who told you that?
> Alice: My mum told me that Jesus was born in Dunstable.
> Geraldine: In a stable!

The Vicar of Dibley

I do benefits for all religions. I'd hate to blow the hereafter on a technicality.

Bob Hope

I would never want to be a member of a group whose symbol is a guy nailed to two pieces of wood.

George Carlin

I'm confused about the direction of Heaven. It's not up there, because the earth revolves, and sometimes you can go to Hell at 8.30, and Heaven at 12.06.

Lenny Bruce

If religion is the opiate of the people, then the Church of England is the paracetamol.

Jeremy Hardy

If you drop a Bible on a field mouse, it'll kill it. So maybe the Bible's not all good?

Harry Hill

I'm normally not a praying man, but if you're up there, please save me, Superman.

Homer Simpson

Nothing like a little chest pain to restore your faith.

Ray Romano

The Vatican is against surrogate mothers. Good thing they didn't have that rule when Jesus was born.

Elayne Boosler

There's no Church of England fundamentalism. We can't have Church of England fundamentalism: you know, like they have Islamic fundamentalism. Jihad!… Ah-ha… Church of England fundamentalism is impossible because you can't have, "You must have tea and cake with the vicar or you die!"

Eddie Izzard

Frankie Boyle (asked to come up with 'things you don't expect a TV announcer to say'): Tonight's episode of Songs of Praise contains strong language and scenes of a sexual nature.

Mock the Week

Two guys came knocking at my door once and said: "We want to talk to you about Jesus." I said: "Oh, no, what's he done now?"

Kevin McAleer

Years ago, my mother gave me a bullet, and I put it in my breast pocket. Two years after that, I was walking down the street when a berserk Evangelist heaved a Bible out of a hotel room window, hitting me in the chest. The Bible would have gone through my heart if it wasn't for the bullet.

Woody Allen

You never hear in the news, "200 killed today when Atheist rebels took heavy shelling from the Agnostic stronghold in the North."

Doug Stanhope

REMEDIAL SCHOOLS

I live near a remedial school. There is a sign that says: "Slow… children." That can't be good for their self-esteem. But look, of course, on the positive side, they can't read it.

Jimmy Carr

THE RENAISSANCE

Blackadder: To you, Baldrick, the Renaissance was just something that happened to other people, wasn't it?

Blackadder

REPUTATION

I'm the girl who lost her reputation and never missed it.

Mae West

RESPECT

As soon as I arrived in camp they gave me a ten-gun salute – or so they told me on the operating table.

Bob Hope

I have nothing but respect for you, and not much of that.

Groucho Marx

Maybe, just once, someone will call me "Sir" without adding, "You're making a scene."

Homer Simpson

RESURRECTION

Alice: I remember the first time my budgie Carrot died. He came back to life, you know – a bit like Jesus, but with feathers.

The Vicar of Dibley

RETIREMENT AND REDUNDANCY

Victor (on being forced to take early retirement): I've been replaced by a box. It's standard procedure, apparently, for a man my age. The next stage is to stick you inside one.

One Foot In the Grave

I remember my staff asking me when I was going to retire. I said when I could no longer hear the sound of laughter. He said: "That never stopped you before."

Bob Hope

REWARDS

Old King Cole: I'm offering a 50,000-guinea reward for Barnaby's apprehension, dead or alive.
Stan: Can't you make up your mind how you want him?

Laurel and Hardy

RHINOS

I worry about rhinos, me. If rhino horn is an aphrodisiac, then why are they an endangered species?

Jasper Carrott

RIGHTS

I don't think there's any way to know if you have any rights before you're born, but I do know that being born again doesn't entitle you to twice as many.

A Whitney Brown

RIPPED OFF

The last time I came up with an invention, I passed the sketch round the pub and I never got the bit of paper back. Three years later: Microsoft Word for Windows.

Harry Hill

ROMAN NUMERALS

She doesn't understand the concept of Roman numerals. She thought we just fought in World War Eleven.

Joan Rivers

ROMANCE

Miss Jones: It was so romantic, Mr Rigsby: champagne, soft lights, Tchaikovsky in the background…
Rigsby: Oh, was he there too?

Rising Damp

ROUGH TIMES

It's been a rough day. I put on a shirt and a button fell off. I picked up my briefcase, and the handle came off. I'm afraid to go to the bathroom.

Rodney Dangerfield

Man, what a rough night I had. My inflatable girlfriend ran off with my air mattress.

Drew Carey

Norm: It's a dog-eat-dog world, and I'm wearing Milkbone underwear.

Cheers

ROYALTY

Here's a piece about Prince Edward... It says ever since he was a teeeenager Edward has wanted to be in the Hussars. It doesn't say whose arse he's wanted to be in...

Bob Monkhouse

RULES

Mackay: There are only two rules in this prison. One: do not write on the walls. Two: You obey all the rules.

Porridge

RUMOURS

So you know the rumour about Whitney Houston is that she's gay. And I mean, it's just a rumour, but that's good enough for me.

Kathy Griffin

That's a vicious rumour! A rumour started by a few million people.

Milton Berle

RURAL FOLK

you see a family having a nice picnic in a field, with a pond, you plough
the family into the field, fill in the pond, you blow up the tree and use the
leaves to make a dress for your wife who's also your brother.

I'm Alan Partridge

Anyone here from Norwich? GIMME SIX!

Marcus Brigstocke

worked some gigs in the Deep South. Alabama…You talk about Darwin's
waiting room, there are guys in Alabama who are their own father.

Dennis Miller

People think everyone from the South is married to their sister and has seen
a UFO. I tell 'em, "Hell, I'm just dating my sister, and I could swear it wasn't a
weather balloon."

Jeff Foxworthy

RUSSIA

Many people are surprised to hear that we have comedians in Russia,
but they are there. They are dead, but they are there.

Yakov Smirnoff

SAFETY

Arthur: If I asked you where the hell we were, would I regret it?
Ford: We're safe.
Arthur: Oh, good.
Ford: We're in a small galley cabin in one of the spaceships of the Vogon
    Constructor Fleet.
Arthur: Ah, this is obviously some strange use of the word "safe" that
    I wasn't previously aware of.

The Hitchhiker's Guide To the Galaxy

SAME OLD STORY

Frank: It's the same old story: boy finds girl, boy loses girl, girl finds boy, boy
    forgets girl, boy remembers girl, girls dies in a tragic blimp accident over the
    Orange Bowl on New Year's Day.
Jane Spencer: Goodyear?
Frank: No, the worst.

The Naked Gu

SAMPLES

Doctor: Now, take this bottle. You know what to do with it, don't you?
Patient: Yes, sir, I do.
Doctor: Good. There's the ship and I want it finished by Tuesday. And if you find
    that too difficult, you can put the ship in the bottle.

I'm Sorry, I'll Read That Aga

Medical Officer: Now, I want you to fill one of those containers for me.
Fletcher: What, from 'ere?

Porridg

SCHOOL TRIPS TO THE COUNTRY

Miss Haggerd: Oh, but don't you see it raises the problem of sex?
Dr Soaper: I wouldn't dream of bothering you in that way.
Miss Haggerd: No, I meant with the girls. They are likely to come into contact
    with boys.
Dr Soaper: Oh, yes. I don't think that will be a problem. It has been my
    experience that once young people sample the delights of country life and
    the wonders of nature, they just can't get enough of it.
Miss Haggerd: Exactly.

Carry On Campin

SCOTLAND

Chisholm: Hairy Scots, tonight we march north to England!
Secombe: But England's south!

Chisholm: Aye, we're gonna march right round the world and sneak up on them from behind!

The Goon Show

Nobody thought Mel Gibson could play a Scot, but look at him now! Alcoholic and a racist!

Frankie Boyle

SCOUTS

A Scout troop consists of 12 little kids dressed like schmucks following a big schmuck dressed like a kid.

Jack Benny

I don't like the Girl Scouts. I can't trust an adolescent female paramilitary organisation that sells highly addictive baked goods.

John MacLain

SCRABBLE

Albert (challenged about using the word "bum" in a game of Scrabble): My "bum" is the American word for "tramp".
Harold: Well, that is where I've got you, because you can't use any slang or colloquialisms!
Albert: Right, then, I'll stick to me English "bum", and that's the part of your anatomy that swells out of the back of your trousers.

Steptoe and Son

SCREAMS

Listen, someone's screaming in agony. Fortunately I speak it fluently.

Spike Milligan

SEA

I was at sea the other day and loads of meat floated past. It was a bit choppy.

Tim Vine

SEA LIFE

I have the world's largest seashell collection. I keep it scattered on beaches all over the world. Maybe you've seen it?

Steven Wright

SEANCES

I said tipsily, "I know what we can do: why don't we all hold hands and try to get in touch with the living?"

Ronnie Corbett

SECURITY

I have six locks on my door, all in a row. When I go out, I lock every other one. I figure no matter how long somebody stands there picking the locks, they're always locking three.

Elayne Boosler

SEDUCTION

Chico: Have you got a woman in here?
Dr Hugo Hackenbush: If I haven't, I've wasted 30 minutes of valuable time.

The Marx Brothers (A Day At the Races)

George Spiggott: In the words of Marcel Proust – and this applies to any woman in the world – if you can stay up and listen with a fair degree of attention to whatever garbage, no matter how stupid it is, that they're coming out with, till ten minutes past four in the morning... you're in.

Peter Cook and Dudley Moore (Bedazzled)

Sonja: My room at midnight?
Boris: All right. Will you be there too?

Love and Death

SEGRAGATION

Every town has the same two malls; the one white people go to and the one white people used to go to.

Chris Rock

SELF-ASSEMBLY

My daughter's tricycle said, "Some Assembly Required". It came in a jar.

Ray Romano

SELF-CONTROL

I exercise extreme self-control. I never drink anything stronger than gin before breakfast.

W C Fields

SERIOUS

Ted Striker: Surely you can't be serious?
Rumack: I am serious... and don't call me Shirley.

Airplane!

SEX

Alan: Right! Let battle commence!

I'm Alan Partridge

I am always looking for meaningful one-night stands.

Dudley Moore

I'm not into that one-night thing. I think a person should get to know someone and even be in love with them before you use them and degrade them.

Steve Martin

If you can't remember the last time you had sex with a woman, you're either gay or married.

Jeff Foxworthy

Luna: It's hard to believe that you haven't had sex for 200 years.
Miles: Two hundred and four, if you count my marriage.

Sleeper

It's so long since I've had sex I've forgotten who ties up who.

Joan Rivers

The last time I was inside a woman was when I visited the Statue of Liberty.

Woody Allen

Ross: A no-sex pact? I have one of those with every woman in America!

Friends

I have so little sex appeal my gynaecologist calls me Sir.

Joan Rivers

My wife is a sex object. Every time I ask for sex, she objects.

Les Dawson

My wife only has sex with me for a purpose. Last night she used me to time an egg.

Rodney Dangerfield

People think I hate sex. I don't. I just don't like things that stop you seeing the television properly.

Victoria Wood

You know that look women get when they want sex? Me neither.

Drew Carey

I wouldn't mind being the last man on Earth – just to see if all of those girls were telling me the truth.

Ronnie Shakes

Women need a reason to have sex. Men just need a place.

Billy Crystal

I believe that sex is the most beautiful, natural, and wholesome thing that money can buy.

Steve Martin

Frasier (on men): How can we possibly use sex to get what we want? Sex is what we want!

Frasier

For the first time in history, sex is more dangerous than the cigarette afterward.

Jay Leno

Someone once came up to me and asked, "If you could sleep with anyone living or dead, who would it be?" and I said, "Anyone living."

Jimmy Carr

Father: How do you segregate the sexes?
Headmaster: If you must know, I go round at night with a crowbar and prise them apart.

Peter Sellers (Common Entrance)

There's an alley at the back of my house and couples are using it for sexual purposes. So I formed my own personal Neighbourhood Watch just to keep an eye on things. So I sit there at night, holding the curtains open with my free hand.

Frank Skinner

I'm a bad lover. Once I caught a Peeping Tom booing me.

Rodney Dangerfield

Before we make love my husband takes a painkiller.

Joan Rivers

The only way I'd need a pain reliever to enjoy sex is if all of my fantasies came true at the same time.

Drew Carey

If sex is such a natural phenomenon, how come there are so many books on how to?

Bette Midler

I once bought her a book called How To Improve Your Man In Bed. And she got somebody else.

John Dowie

If you run out of KY Jelly, a fine emergency substitute is something called "foreplay".

Jeff Green

Alan: Do you like me doing that? Shall I do it more quickly or shall I maintain the same speed?
Jill: That's fine.
Alan: Right. Shall… er… shall I move on to the other one?

I'm Alan Partridge

Foreplay is like beefburgers – three minutes on each side.

Victoria Wood

During sex, my girlfriend always wants to talk to me. Just the other night she called me from a hotel.

Rodney Dangerfield

I once made love for an hour and 15 minutes, but it was the night the clocks are set ahead.

Garry Shandling

Well, Sonja, that was classic intercourse.

I'm Alan Partridge

A multiple orgasm is like a good music system: something you see in magazines and which other people have.

Jeremy Hardy

After making love, I said to my girl, "Was it good for you too?" And she said, "I don't think this was good for anybody."

Garry Shandling

I was making love to this girl and she started crying. I said, "Are you going to hate yourself in the morning?" She said. "No. I hate myself now."

Rodney Dangerfield

I can't think of anything worse after a night of drinking than waking up next to someone and not being able to remember their name, or how you met, or why they're dead.

Laura Kightlinger

Sex is not that important; it's the afterward part, when you're naked and it's warm. Watching the sun come up through the windshield, you look in her good eye and you help strap on her leg and you know: you fucked a pirate.

Dave Attell

What should one say after making love? "Thank you" seems too much; "I'm sorry", not enough.

Simon Munnery

The woman I broke up with is going round telling all her friends that I gave her an anticlimax.

Richard Lewis

Monica: I can't believe my dad saw us having sex. He didn't make it to one of my piano recitals, but this he sees.

Friends

I believe that sex between two people is a beautiful experience. Between five, it's fantastic!

Woody Allen

A threesome was never a fantasy of mine. What: wake up with TWO disappointed ladies in the morning?

Bobcat Goldthwait

The closest I ever came to a ménage à trois was when I dated a schizophrenic.

Rita Rudner

Ali G: Me Uncle Jamal say that he is tri-sexual: that he will try anything that is sexual.

Ali G

I'd like to meet the man who invented sex and see what he's working on now.

George Carlin

Most of us spend the first six days of each week sowing wild oats; then we go to church on Sunday and pray for a crop failure.

Fred Allen

My classmates would copulate with anything that moved, but I never saw any reason to limit myself.

Emo Philips

I got a letter from my mother: "Since you left home your father has become a sex maniac and tries to make love to me every opportunity he gets. Please excuse the wobbly writing."

Frank Carson

He had ambitions at one time to become a sex maniac, but he failed his practical.

Les Dawson

Sally: Patrick, what do you call people you go out with but don't try to sleep with?
Patrick: Men?

Coupling

Roz: I read somewhere that if you have physical contact on a regular basis, it can actually extend your life.
Frasier: Well, in that case, you should outlive Styrofoam.

Frasier

Sex can lead to nasty things like herpes, gonorrhoea and something called relationships.

Ali G

Sex for an old guy is a bit like shooting pool with a rope.

George Burns

The trouble with life is, by the time you can read a girl like a book, your library card has expired.

Milton Berle

I blame my mother for my poor sex life. All she told me was, "The man goes on top and the woman underneath." For three years my husband and I slept in bunk beds.

Joan Rivers

Sally: Oh...Oh God...Ooo Oh God...Oh...Oh...Oh...Oh God...Oh yeah right there Oh! Oh...Yes Yes Yes Yes Yes Yes...Oh...Oh...Yes Yes Yes....Oh...Yes Yes Yes Yes Yes Yes...Oh...Oh... Oh...Oh God Oh... Oh... Huh...
Old lady at next table: (To waiter) I'll have what she's having.

When Harry Met Sally

SEX AIDS

If they ever invent a vibrator that can open pickle jars, men have had it.

Jeff Green

SEX EDUCATION

In my day we didn't have sex education; we just picked up what we could off the television, and as far as I was concerned, if Pinky and Perky didn't do it, I didn't want to know about it.

Victoria Wood: As Seen On TV

The teacher who took us for sex education was very, very shy. In fact, he was so shy he used to shut himself in a cupboard and shout through a knot-hole.

Ronnie Corbett

My father told me all about the birds and the bees, the liar; I went steady with a woodpecker till I was 21.

Bob Hope

SEXUAL HARASSMENT

Sexual harassment at work; is it a problem for the self-employed?

Victoria Wood: As Seen On TV

Today, the LA Times accused Arnold Schwarzenegger of groping six women. I'm telling you, this guy is presidential material.

David Letterman

SHAKESPEARIAN HUMOUR

Bill Oddie: I say, I say, I say; I sent thee sixpence for thy leman. Hadst it?

Tim Brooke-Taylor: I did impeticos thy gratility; for Malvolio's nose is no whipstock. My lady has a white hand, and the Myrmidons are no bottle-ale houses.

John Cleese: Yes – that's real Shakespeare... so just you be thankful for our jokes, or else we shall do all the Shakespearian comedies, one by one, very slowly, twice.

I'm Sorry, I'll Read That Again

SHEEP

Interviewer: You have two dogs? Where are they now?

Shepherd: Over there by that pile of dead sheep. Magnificent brute – treacherous to a fault. Just has this little weakness for mutton.

Interviewer: Do the dogs kill the sheep?

Shepherd: Only in fun. Still, that's better than burying them in the ground and pulling their heads off; it's more humane.

At Last the 1948 Show

Rustic: 'Tis my belief that these sheep are labouring under the misapprehension that they're birds. First, observe their tendency to 'op about the field on their back legs. Now... witness their attempts to fly from tree to tree. Notice they do not so much fly as plummet.

Monty Python's Flying Circus

SHOES

Pa Glum: Ron, rush upstairs and fetch me your mother's toothbrush. I've got my new suede shoes on and I've trodden in something.

Take It From Here

You get really big trainers these days: the sort of things that Florence used to wear in the Magic Roundabout. I was in a sports shop and this kid was returning a pair of trainers because they were rubbing him under the armpits.

Frank Skinner

If you have a choice of selling shoes to ladies or giving birth to a flaming porcupine... look into that second career.

Richard Jeni

SHOPPING

Do these violent films make us violent? I don't know. I haven't seen any of them and I'm violent, particularly at the January sales. I don't buy anything. I just go round hitting people.

Jo Brand

My wife has a black belt in shopping.

Henny Youngman

The odds of going to the store for a loaf of bread and coming out with ONLY a loaf of bread are three billion to one.

Erma Bombeck

Del (finding the shop they were going to is shut): It's closed!
Trigger: Well, it's a bit late, innit?
Del: What d'you mean "a bit late?" You said it was open 24 hours a day.
Trigger: Yeah, but not at night!

Only Fools And Horses

Today I was arrested for scalping low numbers at the deli. I sold a number three for $50.

Steven Wright

My wife will buy anything marked down. Last year she bought an escalator.

Henny Youngman

Shopping is like sex for men, too. They can only manage it for five minutes and then they get tired.

Jeff Green

SHOWBUSINESS

This is based on Give Us A Clue, the entertainment show that really was something else.

I'm Sorry I Haven't A Clue

I could tell a joke in Newport, it would get a huge laugh. But if I told the same joke in Newmarket it would get nothing. The audience couldn't hear me.

Ken Dodd

I shake my tits a lot. If you don't want to listen, you can just watch.

Bette Midler

Last time I acted, my name was so low on the programme I was getting orders for the printing.

Frank Carson

The party was given to launch his mother in her new showbiz career as a lady fire-eater: something that happened quite by accident when she went to put some coal on the fire and tripped over the mat.

Ronnie Corbett

With the collapse of vaudeville, new talent has no place to stink.

George Burns

SHYNESS

Even when we got married I was so shy that we hardly spoke from the time we shook hands at the altar until I waved to her from the window of my room at the YMCA, Torremolinos.

Ronnie Corbett

I'm too shy to express my sexual needs except over the phone to people
I don't know.

Garry Shandling

SIEGES

Waco. What was that all about? One religious fanatic holding 30 children against
their will. In my day we used to call that Sunday school.

Jo Brand

SILENCE

Silence is not only golden, it's seldom misquoted.

Bob Monkhouse

SINGLE

Why get married and make one man miserable when I can stay single and make
thousands miserable?

Carrie Snow

For the single woman, preparing for company means wiping the lipstick off the
milk carton.

Elayne Boosler

The great thing about being single is that you can do what you want when you
want, and the bad thing is you've got nothing to do and no one to do it with.

James O'Loghlin

I met my wife in one of those singles bars. What a surprise – I thought she was
home watching the kids.

Ron Dentinger

SINS

The wages of sin are death, but by the time taxes are taken out, it's just sort of
a tired feeling.

Paula Poundstone

SIRENS

Eric (after hearing a police siren go by): He's not going to sell much ice-cream going at that speed.

Morecambe and Wise

SIZE

I don't understand the sizes anymore. There's a size zero, which I didn't even know that they had. It must stand for: "Ohhh, my God, you're thin."

Ellen DeGeneres

I went into a clothing store, and the lady asked me what size I was. I said, "Actual. I'm not to scale."

Demetri Martin

People walk up to me and say, "You're not as big as you are on telly, are you?" Well, I don't know. How big's your television?

Jack Dee

You're thinking, "He's a bit of a small bastard, isn't he?" In actual fact, I'm not actually that small because, in proportion to my genitals, I'm quite big.

Jeremy Hardy

SKIN

If we all just peeled off our skins… we'd be in agony. But that's a small price to pay for world unity.

Simon Munnery

SLEEP

When I woke up this morning, my girlfriend asked if I'd slept well. I said, "No, I made a few mistakes."

Steven Wright

Every morning I hear the alarm; it's like "BEEP BEEP BEEP". For a second, I'm like, "I could get used to that: just dream I'm in a techno club, or something."

Jim Gaffigan

Shh, don't wake him up! He's got a bad case of insomnia and he's trying to sleep it off.

Chico Marx

I slept like a log last night. I woke up in a fireplace…

Tommy Cooper

I love sleeping in. That can backfire, though. "Ugh, I got up at 4pm. Great, now when am I supposed to nap? My day's ruined."

Jim Gaffigan

I hate it when my foot falls asleep during the day. It means it's going to be up all night.

Steven Wright

SLOUGH

I was born in Slough in the 1970s. If you want to know what Slough was like in the 1970s, go there now.

Jimmy Carr

SMALL HOUSES

I had a great business plan: I was going to build bungalows for dwarfs. There was only one tiny flaw...

Justin Edwards

Our terraced house was so small the mice walked about on their back legs.

Les Dawson

SMELL

The University of Ilinois has hired 15 women to smell pig manure all day so that researchers can find out what makes pig manure smell so bad. You know who I feel sorry for? The woman who applied for this job and got turned down.

Jay Leno

SMOKING

How much do you smoke, sir? Two packs a day? Is that right? You pussy! I go through two lighters a day.

Bill Hicks

Denise Royle: I'm only not smoking in front of Baby David until he's old enough to get up and walk out of the room. Then it's his choice.

The Royle Family

I'm Bill Hicks and I'm dead now because I smoked cigarettes. Cigarettes didn't kill me; a bunch of non-smokers kicked the shit out of me one day. I tried to run; they had more energy than I. I tried to hide; they heard me wheezing. Many of them smelled me.

Bill Hicks

I'm gonna get one of those tracheotomies, so I can smoke two cigarettes at the same time! I'm gonna get nine tracheotomies, all around my neck. I'll be Tracheotomy Man! He can smoke a pack at a time; he's Tracheotomy Man!

Denis Leary

Smokers who blow smoke in my face will learn first-hand (within minutes, actually) how injurious smoking can be to their health.

Erma Bombeck

They're talking about banning cigarette smoking now in any place that's used by ten or more people in a week, which I guess means that Madonna can't even smoke in bed.

Bill Maher

We all know smoking is bad. I know I'm going to quit some day. If I thought I wasn't, I'd quit now.

Dylan Moran

SOLITARINESS

I think loneliness is a terrible thing, you know. Oh, I do, especially when you're on your own.

Frankie Howerd

Holly: As the days go by, we face the increasing inevitability that we are alone in a godless, uninhabited, hostile and meaningless universe. Still, you've got to laugh, haven't you?

Red Dwarf

SOOTHSAYING

Soothsayer: I will see whether the goddess will grant us a further vision. Oh Isis, sweet Isis...
Hengist Pod: They're lovely. I'm very sorry, sir, it's an old saying we have back in Britain.

Carry On Cleo

SOPPY TALK

Thelma Todd: If icky baby don't learn about the football signals, icky baby gonna cwy.
Groucho: If icky girl keep on talking that way, big stwong man's gonna kick all of her teef wight down her fwoat.

The Marx Brothers (Horse Feathers)

SORT OF

"Sort of" is such a harmless thing to say. Sort of. It's just a filler. Sort of. It doesn't really mean anything. But after certain things, "sort of" means everything: like after "I love you", or "You're going to live", or "It's a boy."

Demetri Martin

SPACE EXPLORATION

After 20 years of research Britain has developed its very own space rocket. The final problem which has occupied scientists for the last few years has now been overcome, and they have designed the perfect launching pad, with the technical assistance of the Milk Marketing Board.

Radio Active

Ali G: When is man going to walk on de sun?
Buzz Aldrin: It's much too hot on the sun. We can never go there.
Ali G: We could go in the winter, when it's colder.

Ali G

> Fred Scuttle: We are going into the outer reaches of the solar plexus, where the unknown man has never set foot. In that! Indestructible the Second!
> Henry McGee: What happened to Indestructible the First?
> Scuttle: It fell apart.

The Benny Hill Show

> Making toast on the moon would be tricky. It's all about timing. If you're not there when it pops, it's goodbye toast.

John MacLain

THE SPANISH INQUISITION

> Religion starts in a groovy place. Someone has an idea but then they die and someone comes in their place and says, "Yes, I agree with these ideas but I'm going to twist them." Like the Spanish Inquisition. It was done in Jesus' name, but I don't remember when Jesus said, "And thou shalt get people and really stretch them to enormously long length..."

Eddie Izzard

> Ximinez: Nobody expects the Spanish Inquisition! Our chief weapon is surprise: surprise and fear... fear and surprise.... Our two weapons are fear and surprise... and ruthless efficiency... Our three weapons are fear, surprise and ruthless efficiency... and an almost fanatical devotion to the Pope... Our four – no. Amongst our weapons... amongst our weaponry... are such diverse elements as fear, surprise... I'll come in again.

Monty Python's Flying Circus

SPARKLERS

> Sparklers are the gay cousins of the fireworks family. I think a flashlight is more dangerous than a sparkler. My friends got M-80s, bottle rockets, ammonium nitrate, manure, a rented van. They're blowing shit up, getting things done. I'm walking around with a sparkler like the Special Olympics torch-boy.

Dave Attell

SPEAKING NICELY

I'll have to apologise for my accent. Well, I say "accent"; this is actually the way words are supposed to be pronounced.

Jimmy Carr

SPEECH IMPEDIMENTS

My wife has a slight impediment in her speech. Every now and then she stops to breathe.

Jimmy Durante

One of my friends has a stutter, and a lot of people think that's a bad thing, but to me that's just like starting certain words with a drum roll. That's not an impediment, that's suspense! What's he going to say? Car?... or Carnival?... Carburetor?

Demetri Martin

SPERM AND SPERM DONATION

Alan Davies: Once they're out, they're alive for 18 hours, so you should leave the telly on if you're going out.

QI

The only truly anonymous donor is the guy who knocks up your daughter.

Lenny Bruce

SPORT

Mrs Merton (to Kris Akabusi): Do you have to plan your tactics before the race or do you just try and run faster than the other blokes?

Mrs Merton

A friend got me seats to the World Series. From where I sat, the game was just a rumour.

Henny Youngman

Black people dominate sports in the United States: 20 per cent of the population and 90 per cent of the final four.

Chris Rock

Don't talk to me about Luton Town Football Club. We now do a lap of honour when we get a corner.

Morecambe and Wise

I used to play football in my youth. Then my eyes went bad. That's why I became a referee.

Morecambe and Wise

If a man watches three football games in a row, he should be declared legally dead.

Erma Bombeck

I asked my old man if I could go ice-skating on the lake. He told me, "Wait 'til it gets warmer."

Rodney Dangerfield

Alan Partridge: Eat my goal! The goalie has got football pie all over his shirt!

The Day Today

SPOTS

It gets Arthur down, being so spotty, and he saw an advertisement which said, "Are you spotty? Are you very spotty? Are you unbelievably spotty? Tick in the right box and enclose five shillings." So he wrote in saying, "I am almost unbelievably spotty. I enclose five shillings." And he got a letter back saying, "Bad luck." That's all he had out of them.

Peter Cook

STAIRLIFTS

I saw an advert for stairlifts once, and it gave you all the info and everything. Then it said, "And when you don't need it any more, we'll buy it back off you!" which basically means when you're dead.

Sean Lock

STAR TREK

Captain Kink: Scotty, you take the lift down to the engine room.
Mr Scott: But it's awful heavy, Captain.

I'm Sorry, I'll Read That Again

There were no Latin people on Star Trek. This was proof that they weren't planning to have us around for the future.

John Leguizamo

STATIONERY

I bought a $7 pen because I always lose pens and I got sick of not caring.

Mitch Hedberg

I saw a stationery store move.

Jay London

STATISTICS

Oh, people can come up with statistics to prove anything, Kent. Fourteen per cent of people know that.

Homer Simpson

USA Today has come out with a new survey; apparently three out of four people make up 75 per cent of the population.

David Letterman

STATUS SYMBOLS

They moved to the suburbs and they have all kinds of status symbols. They have their own home and stationwagon and fire insurance and life insurance and mutual funds and his wife has orgasmic insurance or something. If her husband fails to satisfy her sexually, Mutual of Omaha has to pay her every month.

Woody Allen

STOKE NEWINGTON

I'm a gossip columnist on What's On In Stoke Newington. You might have seen it; it's a big piece of paper with "Fuck All" written on it.

Alexei Sayle

STORMING OUT

Niles: And I stormed out and slammed the door! Of course, it was that fourteenth-century Bavarian cathedral door, so I had to get two of the servants to help me, but what it lacked in spontaneity it made up for in resonance.

Frasier

STRENGTHS AND WEAKNESSES

Brent (going through the form Keith has filled in for his appraisal interview): Under "Strengths", you've just put "Accounts".
Keith: Yeah.
Brent: That's your job,though; that's just… that's just… under "Weaknesses" you've put "Eczema".

The Office

STUDENTS

If you've never met a student from the University of Chicago, I'll describe him to you. If you give him a glass of water, he says, "This is a glass of water. But is it a glass of water? And if it is a glass of water, why is it a glass of water?" And eventually he dies of thirst.

Shelley Berman

STUFFED ANIMALS

Stuffed deer-heads on walls are bad enough, but it's worse when they're
wearing dark glasses and have streamers in their antlers because then
you know they were enjoying themselves at a party when they were shot.

Ellen DeGeneres

SUCCESS AND FAILURE

George: What kind of a person are you?
Jerry: I think I'm pretty much like you, only successful.

Seinfeld

Behind every successful man is a woman; behind her is his wife.

Groucho Marx

How about those people who don't need sleep; what are they called again?
Successful? What a bunch of dicks they are.

Jim Gaffigan

If at first you don't succeed, try again. Then quit. There's no use being
a damn fool about it.

W C Fields

If at first you don't succeed... so much for skydiving.

Henny Youngman

Max Bialystock: I'm condemned by a society that demands success when
all I can offer is failure!

The Producers

She said I was afraid of success, which may in fact be true, because I have a
feeling that fufilling my potential would really cut into my sittin' around time.

Maria Bamford

SUICIDE

George Spiggott: You realise that suicide's a criminal offence? In less enlightened times they'd have hung you for it.

Peter Cook and Dudley Moore (Bedazzled)

Suicide is man's way of telling God: "You can't fire me; I quit!"

Bill Maher

SUMO

I was watching what I thought was sumo wrestling on the television for two hours before I realised it was darts.

Hattie Hayridge

SUNBATHING

I'm a bit wan because there hasn't been much sun this year, but I don't cheat with lamps and creams. I don't use fake tan. I think I might Tippex my abdomen to make the rest of me look darker.

Jeremy Hardy

I'm redheaded and fair-skinned, and when I go to the beach, I don't tan; I stroke.

Woody Allen

SURVIVAL

Ed: Doctors say that Nordberg has a 50-50 chance of living, though there's only a ten per cent chance of that.

The Naked Gun

Once, in the wilds of Afghanistan, I lost my corkscrew, and we were forced to live on nothing but food and water for days.

W C Fields

SWEARING

I have a jar at home, and I put pennies in it whenever I curse. The other day I spilled the jar. I owe it about $25.

Demetri Martin

I've been accused of vulgarity. I say that's bullshit.

Mel Brooks

People say profanity comes from lack of vocabulary. That's not true. I know at least at 127 words and I still prefer "fuck".

Billy Connolly

SWEDEN

I've been to Sweden. I found the people there very friendly, kind, trusting people. It makes shoplifting a piece of piss, it really does.

Jack Dee

SWIMMING

So I rang up my local swimming baths. I said, "Is that the local swimming baths?" He said, "It depends where you're calling from."

Tim Vine

Swimming is good for you, especially if you're drowning. Not only do you get a cardiovascular workout but you also don't die.

Jimmy Carr

Seagoon: As I swam ashore, I dried myself to save time.

The Goon Show

Tom Baker: Swimming pools in Britain have very strict rules: no bombing, no petting, no ducking and no fondue parties.

Little Britain

SWITZERLAND

Look at the situation the Swiss have got themselves into. They've got the French to the left of them; Austrians to the right of them; Germans up above; Italians down below. You'd never sell that flat, would you?

Al Murray (The Pub Landlord)

TARTAN

Scottish-Americans tell you that if you want to identify tartans, it's easy. You look under the kilt and if it's a quarter-pounder, it's a McDonald's!

Billy Connolly

TATTOOS

I always look for a woman who has a tattoo. I see a woman with a tattoo, and I'm thinking: "OK; here's a gal who's capable of making a decision she'll regret in the future."

Richard Jeni

I want to get a tattoo over my entire body of myself, but taller.

Steven Wright

My Nan has a picture of the United Kingdom tattooed all over her body. You can say what you like about my Nan, but at least you know where you are with her.

Harry Hill

The other day, I got a henna tattoo that says: "Forever".

Zach Galifianakis

What's the point of getting a tattoo on the inside of your lip unless it says: "Cheer up"?

Adam Bloom

TAX

Everyone should pay their income tax with a smile. I tried it, but they demanded cash.

Jackie Mason

He's spending a year dead for tax purposes.

Douglas Adams

Last year, I deducted 10,697 cartons of cigarettes as a business expense.
The tax man said, "Don't ever let us catch you without a cigarette in your hand."

Dick Gregory

The current tax code is harder to understand than Bob Dylan reading Finnegan's
Wake in a wind tunnel.

Dennis Miller

TCHAIKOVSKY

Pete (Peter Ilyich Tchaikovsky) was born in Votkinsk, May 7, 1840. When
he was a little boy he never played out in the streets of Votkinsk like the
other little children of Votkinsk because when Tchaikovsky was one month
old his parents moved to St Petersburg.

Victor Borge

TEA

Mrs Doyle (offering a nice cup of tea): What would you say to a cup, Father?
Father Jack Hackett: FECK OFF, CUP!

Father Ted

TEACHING MEN

Don't try to teach men how to do anything in public. They can learn in private; in
public they have to know.

Rita Rudner

TECHNOLOGY

A federal judge has ruled that Microsoft should be split into two different
companies. One company will have the Windows operating system
and the other will count Bill Gates' money.

Conan O'Brien

I have a microwave fireplace. I can lie down in front of the fire for the evening in eight minutes.

Steven Wright

It is only when they go wrong that machines remind you how powerful they are.

Clive James

TEENAGERS

Remember that as a teenager, you are in the last stage of your life when you will be happy to hear the phone is for you.

Fran Lebowitz

TEFLON

If nothing sticks to Teflon, what makes it stick to the pan?

Gallagher

TELEVISION

Archie Bunker: Entertainment is a thing of the past; today we've got television.

All In the Family

I don't watch television; I think it destroys the art of talking about oneself.

Stephen Fry

Television is a medium because anything well done is rare.

Fred Allen

The other day a woman came up to me and said: "Didn't I see you on television?" I said: "I don't know. You can't see out the other way."

Emo Philips

Hugh Dennis (asked to come up with 'things you don't expect a television announcer to say'): If you've been affected by the issues raised in Balamory...

Mock the Week

TERRORISM

I don't worry about terrorism. I was married for two years.

Sam Kinison

I'd like to thank the Americans for their help in the War Against Terror, because if you hadn't funded the IRA for 30 years, we wouldn't know how to deal with terrorists, would we?

Al Murray (The Pub Landlord)

The Provisional IRA have admitted responsibility for the Irish entry in the Eurovision Song Contest.

Not the Nine O'Clock News

The last terrorist act we pulled, we planted a fish soup aboard a jumbo jet, and we told them if it wasn't eaten within 24 hours it would go off. And it did.

Not The Nine O'Clock News

The only people flying to Europe will be terrorists, so it will be: "Will you be sitting in armed or unarmed?"

Robin Williams

If the terrorists hated freedom, then the Netherlands would be fucking dust.

David Cross

When Joan Rivers has her make-up confiscated by airport security, even the terrorists will have realised that they have made a huge mistake.

Conan O'Brien

THANKSGIVING

I celebrated Thanksgiving in an old-fashioned way. I invited everyone in my neighbourhood to my house, we had an enormous feast, and then I killed them and took their land.

Jon Stewart

THE NATURAL WORLD

Lister: Love is what separates us from animals.
Rimmer: No, Lister. What separates us from animals is that we don't use our tongues to clean our own genitals.

Red Dwarf

Animals may be our friends, but they won't pick you up at the airport.

Bobcat Goldthwait

Stephen Fry: What do you get when you cross a camel with a leopard?
Jo Brand: Is it a fireside rug you can have a good hump on?
Sean Lock: You get sacked from the zoo?

QI

I saw this bloke chatting up a cheetah. I thought: "He's trying to pull a fast one."

Tim Vine

Stephen Fry: How do otters kill crocodiles?
Rob Brydon: Softly with their songs.

QI

Stephen Fry: What's the collective noun for a group of baboons?
Rich Hall: The Pentagon.

QI

THEATRE

I go to the theatre to be entertained. I want to be taken out of myself. I don't want to see lust and rape, incest and sodomy. I can get all that at home.

Beyond the Fringe

Max Bialystock (after his guaranteed flop production has proved to be a hit): How could this happen? I was so careful. I picked the wrong play, the wrong director, the wrong cast. Where did I go right?

The Producers

The secret of acting is sincerity. If you can fake that, you've got it made.

George Burns

This stage, if it hasn't done so already, will at some point stage a performance of The Vagina Monologues, which I have to see, just because it sounds so fabulously stupid. Everybody knows that if female genitalia could speak, it would sound exactly like Enya.

Dylan Moran

THINKING

Rose: You know what I think?
Blanche: No, do you?

The Golden Girls

Joey: I thought it'd be great, you know: have some time alone with my thoughts? Turns out I don't have as many thoughts as you'd think.

Friends

Stan: You know, Ollie, I was just thinking.
Ollie: About what?
Stan: Nothing. I was just thinking.

Laurel and Hardy

Alex: It's so quiet up here you can hear yourself think.
Reverend Jim: I don't hear anything.

Taxi

Frasier: My study? You expect me to give up my study? The place where I read, where I do my most profound thinking?
Martin: Ah, use the can like the rest of the world!

Frasier

Why do women insist on asking men what they're thinking? We're thinking: "Fuck, better think of something to say." Either that or we're imagining that we're spies.

Ed Byrne

THREATS

Eddie: Richard, I'm warning you. If you don't shut up and let me watch Miss World I'm going to stuff your head up your bum, and you'll spend the rest of your life wandering around on all fours looking for the light switch.

Bottom

I'd just like to say to the old man wearing camouflage gear and using crutches who stole my wallet earlier: "You can hide, but you can't run."

Milton Jones

Sybil: You know what I'll do if I find out that money is yours?
Basil: You'd have to sew 'em back on first.

Fawlty Towers

The Mafia people appeal to your intellect: "You're an intelligent person, aren't you? So you realise it's very difficult to walk without knees."

Richard Pryor

The temperature inside this apple pie is over 1,000 degrees. If I squeeze it, a jet of molten Bramley apple will squirt out. Could go your way; could go mine. Either way, one of us is going down!

I'm Alan Partridge

You won't be laughing when my medication wears off.

Lily Savage

TIME

Ford: Time is an illusion; lunchtime doubly so.

The Hitchhiker's Guide To the Galaxy

Men love watches that have multiple functions. My husband has one that is a combination address book, telescope and piano.

Rita Rudner

Time flies like an arrow. Fruit flies like a banana.

Groucho Marx

TIREDNESS

I saw a sign by the side of the road that said: "Tiredness can kill." I never knew that. Last Saturday I stayed up watching films! I could have died!

Ardal O'Hanlon

Prince Charles has regretted the outcry over his use of the word "knackered" to describe his condition, and says next time he feels shagged out he'll keep his gob shut.

Not the Nine O'Clock News

TOAST

If toast always lands butter-side-down, and cats always land on their feet, what happens if you strap toast on the back of a cat and drop it?

Steven Wright

TOILETS

Do you know what this bathroom says to me? Aqua, which is French for water. It's like being inside an enormous Fox's Glacier Mint, which, again, to me is a bonus.

I'm Alan Partridge

Jerry: There's too much urinary freedom in this society. I'm proud to hold it in. It builds character.

Seinfeld

Jim Royle (coming back from the toilet): Woah-ho, if you lot take my advice, you won't go near that lavatory for at least half an hour, and whatever you do, don't strike a bloody match.

The Royle Family

Marty Funkhouser: Why do you pee sitting down?
Larry David: Many reasons.
Funkhouser: Do you crap standing up?

Curb Your Enthusiasm

Men who consistently leave the toilet seat up secretly want women to get up to go to the bathroom in the middle of the night and fall in.

Rita Rudner

I do like that toilet. It's very futuristic, isn't it? Very sort of high-tech, space-age. I can imagine Buck Rogers taking a dump on that, in the twenty-first century.

I'm Alan Partridge

Red Baron: How lucky you English are to find the toilet so amusing. For us, it is a mundane and functional item. For you, it is the basis of an entire culture.

Blackadder

You can say, "Can I use your bathroom?" and nobody cares, but if you ask, "Can I use the plop-plop machine?" it always breaks the conversation.

Dave Attell

TOYS

I could tell that my parents hated me. My bath toys were a toaster and a radio.

Rodney Dangerfield

TRAVEL

Another travel agent told me I could spend seven nights in Hawaii: no days, just nights.

Rodney Dangerfield

Kenneth Horne: Hmm. I'll think about it. But tell me, what brought you into the travel business in the first place?
Julian: Well, we've always enjoyed cruising, haven't we, Sand?

Round the Horne

TRAVELLERS

In the 1968 Caravan Sites Act, gipsies are defined as "persons constantly travelling, never in one place for more than few weeks." Which means that, technically, the Duchess of York is a gipsy.

Have I Got News For You

TROUSER PRESS

The Corby trouser press: don't it hurt your legs?

Lee Evans

TRUTH

Frank Drebin: The truth hurts doesn't it, Hapsburg? Oh, sure, maybe not as much as jumping on a bicycle with the seat missing, but it hurts.

The Naked Gun

TWINS

Tragically, I was an only twin.

Peter Cook

I'm writing a book about Siamese twins that are attached at the nose. It's called, Stop Staring at Me!

Zach Galifianakis

TYPING

I type at 101 words a minute, but it's in my own language.

Mitch Hedberg

UGLINESS

I'm so ugly. I worked in a pet shop, and people kept asking how big I'd get.

Rodney Dangerfield

How would you like to feel the way she looks?

Groucho Marx

Jonathan Ross: What's the protocol for when you see a really ugly baby?
Rich Hall: I'll tell you. People show you their babies on their phone now, and it's like a cashew with some hair coming out of it. The thing to say is, "Nice phone".

QI

Last week I saw my psychiatrist and told him I kept thinking I was ugly. He told me to lie on the couch, face-down.

Rodney Dangerfield

She looked like a ten-pound bag of shite in a two-pound bag.

Lily Savage

Yes, darling, let me cover your face with kisses... on second thoughts, just let me cover your face.

Groucho Marx

I knew a girl so ugly that she was known as a two-bagger. That's when you put a bag over your head in case the bag over her head falls off.

Rodney Dangerfield

UNCARING

Honey, just because I don't care doesn't mean I don't understand!

Homer Simpson

I'm sorry if that came across like I don't care. I don't, so it probably did.

Marcus Brigstocke

UNDERSTANDING

Firefly: Why, a four-year-old child could understand this report. Run out and find me a four-year-old child. I can't make head or tail out of it.

The Marx Brothers (Duck Soup)

UNDERWEAR

Men want the same thing from their underwear that they want from women: a little bit of support and a little bit of freedom.

Jerry Seinfeld

Poor soul. There's nothing worse than your knickers out of focus.

Frankie Howerd

VARICOSE VEINS

She was depressed about the veins on her legs. She'd had shorts on
the other day, and her husband had used her left thigh to direct someone
to the motorway.

Victoria Wood: As Seen On TV

VASECTOMY

I told my doctor I wanted a vasectomy. He said with a face like mine, I don't
need one.

Rodney Dangerfield

VEAL

Jeremy Clarkson: Did you know a veal calf has to have more space to be
transported to the abattoir than a human being in the back of an aeroplane?
Sean Lock: Yeah, but to be fair, we have a holiday; they get killed.

QI

VEGETARIANS

German food is so bad, even Hitler was a vegetarian.

Dylan Moran

I won't eat anything that has intelligent life, but I'd gladly eat a network executive
or a politician.

Marty Feldman

I'm a postmodern vegetarian; I eat meat ironically.

Bill Bailey

I'm a vegetarian. Well, I'm not hardcore because I eat meat, but only because I
like the taste, and I hate vegetables on a personal level, so I'm not too good!

Dylan Moran

I'm not a vegetarian, but I eat animals who are.

Groucho Marx

It's true, Hitler was a vegetarian. It's a cautionary tale. In large doses, it can cause genocide.

Bill Bailey

Our Janine: I've gone vegetarian now. I mean, I know I had a sausage roll yesterday, but it's not really meat, is it, y'know? I mean, there's no animal called a 'sausage'.

The Fast Show

You know, when they sell that tofu? Girls, have you ever had a yeast infection? You know what I'm saying?

Ruby Wax

VERBAL SKILLS

A study in the Washington Post says that women have better verbal skills than men. I just want to say to the authors of that study: duh.

Conan O'Brien

VIAGRA

Old men don't need Viagra because they're impotent. Old men need Viagra because old women are very, very ugly.

Jimmy Carr

The marketers of Viagra have a new slogan, "Let the Dance Begin". This is better than the original, "Brace Yourself, Grandma!"

Jay Leno

VIOLENCE

TV Vicar: It is my aim to get the violence off the streets and into the churches where it belongs.

Jonathan Miller (Beyond the Fringe)

Vyvyan (hitting Rick in the crotch with a cricket bat): Shut your face, traitor!
Rick: Hah! Missed both my legs!

The Young Ones

Experts say you should never hit your children in anger. When is a good time? When you're feeling festive?

Roseanne

My father used to beat me with his belt… while it was still on him.

Zach Galifianakis

Did you hear about the woman who stabbed her husband 37 times? I admire her restraint.

Roseanne

VIRGINS

The only thing Madonna will ever do like a virgin is give birth in a stable.

Bette Midler

Vicky Pollard (on being told that she is pregnant): Yeah but no but yeah but no but yeah but no, because I've never had sex apart from that one time eight months ago, but apart from that I'm a complete virgin.

Little Britain

VITAMINS

I take vitamins. They drop and roll under the refrigerator. I don't pick them up. I have years of vitamins under the refrigerator. I'm going to come home one night and find a six-foot roach saying, "I feel good!"

Elayne Boosler

VOMIT

Stephen Fry: What is a vomitorium?
Phill Jupitus: Is it London's least successful tourist destination?

QI

And vomiting? "Talking tae God on the big white telephone." In Australia they call it, "Driving the porcelain truck."

Billy Connolly

Have you noticed there are always diced carrots in your vomit? I NEVER EAT DICED CARROTS! There must be idiots following drunks and putting diced carrots in their beer when they're not looking.

Billy Connolly

WAISTS

I haven't got a waist. I've just got a sort of place a bit like an unmarked level crossing.

Victoria Wood: As Seen On TV

WALES

A beauty contest for sheep has been put on, somewhat bizarrely, to amaze the crowds at the Welsh Film Festival. Of course, if they'd really wanted to amaze people, they could have just put on a famous Welsh film.

Have I Got News For You

WALKING

I like long walks – especially when they're taken by people who annoy me.

Fred Allen

I was walking along this narrow mountain pass – so narrow that nobody else could pass you – when I saw a beautiful blonde walking towards me. A beautiful blonde with not a stitch on. Yes, not a stitch on, lady. Cor, blimey, I didn't know whether to toss myself off or block her passage.

Max Miller

WAR

All men are brothers: hence war.

Simon Munnery

Basil: Don't mention the war. I mentioned it once, but I think I got away with it all right.

Fawlty Towers

Blackadder: There hasn't been a war run this badly since Olaf the Hairy, King of all the Vikings, ordered 80,000 battle helmets with the horns on the inside.

Blackadder

I feel that if ANY songs are to come out of World War Three, we'd better start writing them now.

Tom Lehrer

President Bush has said that he does not need approval from the UN to wage war, and I'm thinking: "Well, hell, he didn't need the approval of the American voters to become president, either."

David Letterman

Trentino: I am willing to do anything to prevent this war.
Firefly: It's too late. I've already paid a month's rent on the battlefield.

The Marx Brothers (Duck Soup)

I can't forgive the Germans for what they did to my granddad in the last war – passed over for promotion time and time again.

Jimmy Carr

Sometimes I think war is God's way of teaching us geography.

Paul Rodriguez

WATERBOARDING

Waterboarding. That's what America does to its prisoners now. Dunking them in water until they confess. Of course, you have to remember we uncovered a lot of witches that way, so credit where credit's due.

A Whitney Brown

WEAPONS

Experts have spent years developing weapons which can destroy people's lives but leave buildings intact. They're called mortgages.

Jeremy Hardy

Guns don't kill people. People kill people, and monkeys do too (if they have a gun).

Eddie Izzard

Mainwaring: You should consider it an honour and a privilege to use this Lewis gun.
Frazer: If it was a privilege, none of us would ever be getting a look-in.

Dad's Army

They say that guns don't kill people. People kill people. But I think the guns help.

Eddie Izzard

WEATHER

Having a gang-bang in Scotland in the winter is like playing pass the parcel, there's that many layers.

Frankie Boyle

In Minnesota, it's so cold some nights you have to wear two condoms.

Bruce Lansky

In the Bible, God made it rain for 40 days and 40 nights. That's a pretty good summer for us in Wales. That's a hosepipe ban waiting to happen. I was eight before I realised you could take a kagoul off.

Rhod Gilbert

Frankie Boyle (asked, 'If this is the answer, what is the question: Up to 18 months'): How long is a Scottish winter?

Mock the Week

Minnie: What a nice summer evening – typical English.
Henry: Mnk, yes – the rain's lovely and warm.

The Goon Show

WELFARE STATE

Ali G: Why do they call it the welfare state? Is it 'cos it is well fair?
Tony Benn: Well, the welfare state means that you've got national insurance.
Ali G: But unemployment is wicked because you get money for doin' nothing.

Ali G

WELL BEING

Blanche: I treat my body like a temple.
Sophia: Yeah, open to everyone, day or night.

The Golden Girls

WET FLOOR

She saw a sign saying "Wet Floor". So she did!

Joan Rivers

WHEN THE MOON HITS YOUR EYE

If the moon hit your eye like a big pizza pie, it might be amore, but I'd
be more worried about the interplanetary gravitational effects from this
cataclysmic event.

Paul Paternoster

WINE, WOMEN AND SONG

I wanted wine, women and song. I got a drunk woman singing.

Simon Munnery

WINTER SPORTS

Skiing combines outdoor fun with knocking down trees with your face.

Dave Barry

You know what's stupid? Skiing. You get on top of a slippery mountain with
sleds on your feet and you go down... big deal. Try not to, or go up! Now
that'd be a sport for ya!

Gallagher

WORDS OF WISDOM

Although no man is an island, you can make quite an effective raft out of six.

Simon Munnery

Carpe per diem: seize the check.

Robin Williams

Holly: Time is a great healer. Unless it's a rash. Then you're better off with ointment.

Red Dwarf

Honesty may be the best policy, but it's important to remember that apparently, by elimination, dishonesty is the second-best policy.

George Carlin

If you can't laugh at yourself, make fun of other people.

Bobby Slayton

If you had to identify, in one word, the reason why the human race has not achieved, and never will achieve, its full potential, that word would be "meetings".

Dave Barry

In the land of the skunks, he who has half a nose is king.

Chris Farley

It's a cruel world; a man's lucky if he gets out of it alive.

W C Fields

It's a small world... but I wouldn't like to paint it.

Steven Wright

Just because nobody complains doesn't mean all parachutes are perfect.

Benny Hill

Melchett: As private parts to the gods are we; they play with us for their sport.

Blackadder

My aunt used to say, "What you can't see can't hurt you." Well, she died of radiation poisoning a few months back!

Harry Hill

My Dad used to say, "Always fight fire with fire", which is probably why he got thrown out of the the the fire brigade.

Harry Hill

My grandfather always said, "Don't watch your money; watch your health." So one day while I was watching my health, someone stole my money. It was my grandfather.

Jackie Mason

If you can't beat them, arrange to have them beaten.

George Carlin

My mother used to say that there are no strangers, only friends you haven't met yet. She's now in a maximum-security twilight home in Australia.

Dame Edna Everage

No day is so bad it can't be fixed with a nap.

Carrie Snow

Remember – even a clock that's stopped is right twice a day.

Benny Hill

Seize the moment. Remember all those women on the 'Titanic' who waved off the dessert cart.

Erma Bombeck

Son, if you really want something in this life, you have to work for it. Now quiet! They're about to announce the lottery numbers.

Homer Simpson

Stan: You can lead a horse to water, but a pencil must be led.

Laurel and Hardy

The day after tomorrow is the third day of the rest of your life.

George Carlin

The pen is mightier than the sword, and considerably easier to write with.

Marty Feldman

The way I see life is like we're all flying on the Hindenburg: why fight over the window seats?

Richard Jeni

When all else fails, there's always self-delusion.

Conan O'Brien

When you see the hand-writing on the wall, you're in the toilet.

Redd Foxx

You can't have everything. Where would you put it?

Steven Wright

You tried your best and you failed miserably. The lesson is: never try.

Homer Simpson

The bigger they are, the worse they smell.

George Carlin

WORK

Brent: I've tried to create an atmosphere where I'm a friend first, boss second, probably entertainer third.

The Office

Larry (to his wife, Cheryl): You don't work. You're unemployed.
Cheryl: Loving you is my job, Larry.

Curb Your Enthusiasm

I've worked myself up from nothing to a state of extreme poverty.

Groucho Marx

Archie Bunker: In 50 years, he never worked a day. To him, nine to five was odds on a horse.

All In the Family

The Chancellor has announced new plans for shortening the dole queues. He's asking the men to stand closer together.

The Two Ronnies

The trouble with the rat race is that even if you win, you're still a rat.

Lily Tomlin

Lisa, if you don't like your job you don't strike. You just go in every day and do it really half-assed. That's the American way.

Homer Simpson

Adults are always asking little kids what they want to be when they grow up because they're looking for ideas.

Paula Poundstone

Well, we can't stand around here doing nothing. People will think we're workmen.

Spike Milligan

YEAST EXTRACT

But I'm in a great mood tonight because the other day I entered a competition and I won a year's supply of Marmite... one jar.

Tim Vine

YOGURT

This is the news that the EU wants to replace the word "yogurt" with the phrase "mild alternate-culture heat-treated fermented milk". By the time you've asked for it, your thrush has cleared up all by itself.

Have I Got News For You

ZIPS

The man who invented the zip fastener was today honoured with a lifetime peerage. He'll now be known as the Lord of the Flies.

The Two Ronnies

ZOOS

When I was a boy, I said, "Daddy, take me to the zoo." My father said, "Son, when the zoo wants you, they'll come and get you."

Fred Allen

In The End...

Peter Cook (among a group gathered on a mountain top awaiting the end
    of the world): Five – four – three – two – one – zero!
All: Now is the end! Perish the world!
(Pause)
Peter: It was GMT, wasn't it? Well, it's not quite the conflagration I'd b
    een banking on. Never mind, lads, same time tomorrow. We must
    get a winner one day.

Beyond the Fringe

GOOD NIGHT

George: Say goodnight, Gracie.
Gracie: Goodnight, Gracie.

George Burns and Gracie Allen